CHAOS OR CREATION

Spirituality in Mid-Life

L. Patrick Carroll, S.J.
Katherine Marie Dyckman, S.N.J.M.

D1113506

Paulist Press
New York/Mahwah

Library of Congress Cataloging-in-Publication Data

Carroll, L. Patrick, 1936–
    Chaos or creation.

    Bibliography: p.
    1. Middle age--Religious life. 2. Spiritual life--
Catholic authors. I. Dyckman, Katherine Marie,
1931–   . II. Title.
BV4579.5.C37   1986   248.4'8204   86-15067
ISBN 0-8091-2832-2 (pbk.)

Published by Paulist Press
997 Macarthur Boulevard
Mahwah, New Jersey 07430

Printed and bound in the
United States of America

Contents

Acknowledgements

We offer our deepest thanks to Sr. Phyllis Taufen, S.N.J.M. who spent many hours proofreading our manuscript; the mistakes are ours despite her finest efforts.

Thanks also to Mary Romer-Cline who typed the final manuscript. Others have word-processors; we only have friends.

Finally, thanks to everyone who has been part of our classes on mid-life spirituality the past four years. Through their reflections and encouragement we found the time to finish this because they found it helpful.

L. Patrick Carroll, S.J.
Katherine Marie Dyckman, S.N.J.M.

Introduction

"I tell you most solemnly,
when you were young
you put on your own belt
and walked where you liked;
but when you grow old
you will stretch out your hands,
and somebody else will put a belt around you
and take you where you would rather not go. . . ."
After this he said: "Follow me" (Jn 21:18–19).[1]

This simple text, almost the final lines of the final Gospel, outline the contents of this book. We will return to them at the end, but here at the outset we suggest that the spirituality of mid-life involves being led by another, a surrendering, a following, a giving-up, and beyond all possible imagining—a receiving.

After these initial words we invite you to pause for a moment and consider some simple questions: Why did you pick up this book? What are you hoping for? What are the issues that perhaps touch you in the middle of your life . . . or as you look forward . . . or look backward? Where are you dying? Where rising? And how is your God involved in your experience?

Having listened to the religious question, hear the same reflection put in psychological terms:

Wholly unprepared, they embark upon the second half of life. Or are there perhaps colleges for forty year olds

1

which prepare them for their coming life and its demands as the ordinary colleges introduce our young
people to a knowledge of the world and of life? No, there
are none. Thoroughly unprepared we take the step into
the afternoon of life: worse still, we take this step with
the false presupposition that our truths and ideals will
serve us as hitherto. But we cannot live the afternoon of
life according to the programme of life's morning; for
what was great in the morning will be little at evening,
and what in the morning was true will at evening have
become a lie.[2]

Though we cannot provide a college, issue a degree, or
even give credits for the work you do, we want to offer reflections, avenues of hope, invitations to growth and life and
laughter to religious people searching in the middle of your
lives. We will provide a variety of ways to view our rather
common, yet unique experience, to offer words or name
feelings, and prayers to express longings. We will not give
you answers, but may provide some way to live with the
questions—questions which, though not unavoidable, risk
spiritual, psychological, and human disaster when skirted.

For centuries the Christian tradition has spoken of the
"dark night of the soul," or "dark contemplation," or a
"cloud of unknowing," in books and language seemingly re-
served for the cloistered monk or nun. Only lately have we
begun to realize that something of this passage occurs in
the life of every human person, at least within the Christian
context (and we suspect in others as well).

In our more recent past, whole bookshelves are filled
with best sellers on the mid-life crisis, the crisis of limits,
the second journey, the male-menopause, or women's coming of age. Since the time of Carl Jung, with words such as
those in the preceding Jungian quote, no topic has so

captured the imagination of contemporary men and women.

Our aim in this book is to bring these apparently separate realities together, to see the religious and the psychological journeys as the single path they truly are. We contend that the religious can learn from the psychological, and that the psychological without the dimension of faith is inadequate to describe the human task. We employ sources from both arenas, interspersed with large doses of human experience—our own, and that of many people we know as friends, retreatants, companions in spiritual direction these past fifteen years and more.

Part I of this book constructs the problem or opportunity. We suggest initial impressions of our shared mid-life experiences—from poetry, drama, novel and film, and from the actual experiences and words of real people. Then from a variety of social scientists, people working in psychology and developmental theory, we suggest a variety of ways to view the situation of human life at its mid-point.

In Part II we look at the identical issues from a different angle and view the same reality as a "faith" reality, seeing through the eyes of Sacred Scripture and some poets of our religious tradition. Then, in a somewhat more programmatic fashion, we reflect on the significant work of James Fowler, because he allows us to see human development as a development of and in faith.

We aim in each of these two parts at surrounding and expounding the experiences of mid-life, offering varied ways or models to examine our experience, providing a way to talk about, to feel, to understand.

In Part III we will try not so much to solve the problems or issues raised as to suggest some ways toward constructively coping, even thriving in the face of our brokenness. Each of the signs and challenges of mid-life which crawled crab-like from beneath their rocks in the first two parts will, in the third, be loved into some kind of life.

In Part IV we deal especially with the questions of prayer at mid-life, for prayer is the only means of transforming our brokenness. We rely again on some of the giants of our tradition (Teresa of Avila, John of the Cross, Meister Eckhart, Thomas Merton, and, more recently, Ruth Burrows), but we rely also on our own experience and the equally valuable prayer lives of ordinary people like ourselves and you.

Our efforts end, as our lives must, in Part V, with a meditation on Jesus and the cross, and the transforming power of that cross, his and ours, into life . . . not only at the end but all the way along.

This, then, is our road map. Join us for the journey. We are not experts, but companions who believe that for the pioneer traveling toward the kingdom of God, the only sin is turning back and leaving others to face the perils alone. When Jesus suggests to Peter that the next stage of his life will be less under his own control, more in the hands of another, the most significant line is his "Follow me!" This very following looks and feels like chaos but can creatively lead to wholeness. We do not go alone, abandoned neither by God nor by one another. We walk with each other a shared, perilous, but ultimately rewarding path.

Notes

1. *The Jerusalem Bible,* London: Darton, Longman and Todd, 1966. We use the Jerusalem Bible translation, unless otherwise noted. At times we choose to render what is essentially this trans-

lation into inclusive language; parentheses indicate the change in text where this occurs.

2. C.G. Jung, *The Collected Works*, R.F.C. Hull, trans. Bollingen series XX, Princeton, N.J., Princeton U. Press, 2nd ed., 1969, Vol. 8, "The Structures and Dynamic of the Psyche," Par. 784, pp. 398–99.

PART I

The Mid-Life Experience

1

Impressions of the Experience

In the middle of his life, T.S. Eliot penned what is perhaps his finest poem, "The Love Song of J. Alfred Prufrock."[1] The Italian lines that preface this poem, lines from Dante's *Inferno* (a poem also written in the middle of that great poet's life), set the tone of profound mid-life hopelessness. "Love Song," and "J. Alfred Prufrock" ironically suggest the impossibility of "love" in the experience of one so named and so bored by the life he has hidden under. Prufrock experiences the futility of the life he is living, where "in the room the women come and go, talking of Michelangelo." He has "known them all, already, known them all—the . . . evenings, mornings, afternoons"; he has "measured out his life in coffee spoons." And because he has been buried by this chosen, but now unwanted life, he feels paralyzed, unable to choose another life, another way of being in the world. He suffers the curse of the once-born, who could not possibly presume to be different. For if he tried, someone who had known him forever, who knew what he was like now and would always be, would tell him, "That's not it at all."

Prufrock is a kind of "Every-(middle-aged)-man" who knows who he is or at least has become—not Hamlet, not a prophet like John the Baptist, but more Petronius, the "fool." His dreams of significance, romance, passions, adventure, have puffed away in London's fog, and he has, in perhaps the poem's most poignant lines, "seen the eternal footman hold my coat, and snicker, / and, in short, I was afraid." Facing his own meaningless mortality, his own crushed dreams, the final dying embers of a chance (but hardly a real chance) to break away, Prufrock is unable to dare change even the part of his hair, or to risk eating a (perhaps unripe?) peach. He images himself growing rapidly older, hunched, his rolled trousers dragging upon the ground, having died many years before his burial takes place, with no mermaid's song for him.

"The Love Song of J. Alfred Prufrock" presents the tragic if underplayed song of one who has failed to make, or even to try to make, the mid-life transition. He epitomizes one who, seeing the emptiness of a life that has been handed him, a life chosen with something less than full consciousness, is afraid and unable to rechoose, to begin again, or to start anew. He touches us because we can see ourselves "wearing the bottom of our trousers rolled," as we hunch our way to premature senility and death. No one captures the innate possibility of futility in mid-life more vividly than Eliot.

Eliot's "Journey of the Magi"[2] plays a different variation on the same theme. Written about the same time as "Prufrock," "The Journey of the Magi" speaks in the voice of a wise man in Matthew's infancy narrative. This "wise man" did have a chance to get out, escape futility, find meaning and new direction to his life. He retells his story, his discovery of the child in the cave of Bethlehem, and "it was (you may say) satisfactory." He manages to escape and walk away from this new birth—not just of a child but of himself and his friends. But one can never go back, and he is "no longer at ease here, in the old dispensation, / with an alien people clutching their gods."

In this most specific poem, Eliot senses the dis-ease of whole generalities of people who have had their chance, seen the vision, risked the adventure, and then, being "king," or "queen," in some other place, turned back to try to find solace in the familiar, the comfortable, the known. When the death of new birth comes, there is no turning back.

From a more feminine perspective, Kathleen Raine, in a less familiar poem, "Northumbrian Sequence IV,"[3] speaks of a part of woman's mid-life experience. The poem offers a kind of prayer inviting into her mid-life all the demons she had thus far successfully kept at bay: wind, rain, fear, pain, the "nameless formless power / that beats upon my door." She invites, despite her ingrained reluctance, a whole host of "shadow" figures, ancestors, unfulfilled desire—"the dead." Unsure that her "virgin" heart can "conceive gigantic solitude," she wrestles with the mid-life need to be in, and be peaceful with, solitude, radical aloneness. She speaks of taking "pity on the raging storm," making friends with that dark self in us all. She longs to let in fire, power, invading might—strong "masculine" images for a woman letting a whole new side of herself emerge, yet still "gentle must my fingers be, and pitiful my heart," for she must not lose her "femininity" in the process.

The poem struggles with ironical combinations of violence and peace, and this woman's desire to hold together the tensions created by both. Her final lines:

Let in the wound,
Let in the pain,
Let in the child tonight,

bring to mind the Jungian archetype of individuation in which the "child" symbolizes the successful adult integration.

With singularly "right-brain" imagery, Raine suggests a host of womb-like impressions conceiving within oneself and bringing forth new life—a psychological rather than biological giving birth characterizing both women and men at mid-life.

Another woman poet, May Sarton, writing in the middle of her life, captures the image of death and life so close together. In her poem "Annunciation" Sarton speaks about Mary but the words apply to all of us:

> . . . So the child leaves the parent torn at birth.
> No one is perfect here, no one is well:
> It is a time of fear and immolation.
> First the hard journey down again to death
> Without a saving word or a free breath,
> And then the terrible annunciation:
> And we are here alone upon the earth. . . .
>
> Nothing at all but to believe and bear,
> Nothing but to foresee that in the ending
> Would lie the true beginning and the birth,
> And all be broken down before the mending.
> For there can never be annunciation
> Without the human heart's descent to Hell.
> And no ascension without the fearful fall. . . .

No one captures the chaos or creation theme of mid-life and of this book better than May Sarton.[4]

This theme of mid-life transition runs rampant in books and movies. The third of John Updike's marvelous "Rabbit" series, *Rabbit Is Rich*, offers a wonderful mid-life glimpse of this anti-hero. The former irresponsible youth (*Rabbit Run*) and upwardly mobile man-about-town (*Rabbit Redux*) finds himself now buried in establishment living, establishment values. Harry Angstrom has made it as a car salesman. His ever-shaky marriage is more stable than imaginable. He even belongs to a golf club! He cannot understand the slovenly, uncommitted life of his son. Though Harry has every material reason for happiness, he is restless with his roots so deep, his life so predictable. If anyone should not have had a mid-life crisis it is Rabbit. Could he not be complacent with suburbia after the chaos of his earlier life? But no, the mid-life hero too must wrestle with his "last chance" feelings of waning sexual prowess, must re-examine, re-evaluate, rebuild what was so precariously accomplished in his previous years.

Bergman's fine film, *Face to Face,* tells the story of Jenny, a woman psychiatrist, separated from her husband who has so far managed her life with almost total professional and personal control. Confronted with both the lack of control and the painful wisdom in a psychotic patient, Jenny faces herself in a kind of distorted-mirror image in the middle of her life. Her patient, Maria, tells her:

> "Do you know what's so incredibly wrong with you? Well, I'll tell you because I've figured it out. *You're unable to love.* . . . You're almost unreal. I've tried to like you as you are because I thought then she'll become a little more real, I mean less anxious and more sure of herself. . . . But not a hope! Jenny looks at me with her lovely big blue eyes, the most beautiful eyes in the world, and all I see is her anguish. Have you ever loved *anybody* Jenny?"[5]

Jenny collapses, suffers her own breakdown. Out of the depth of her own psychological death, she recognizes the emptiness of her life so far, perceives the need to live authentically with integrity as the person she truly is—not a role, a shell, an empty professional woman. She discovers, out of this mid-life disintegration, a new way of being in interdependence with others and with God. This commonality with the illness of her patient, the shared suffering that replaces her habitual "taking care of," begins both death and new life for her. Giving up control or its illusion, she emerges more whole than she has ever been. Somehow in giving up, she receives a new and better life.

Staying for a moment with the psychological, the play/ movie *Equus* of a few years ago tells a wrenching story that, at first glance, seemed to be about a young man who in a fit of irrational behavior had maimed several horses, stabbing out their eyes. Upon probing, one feels that the story focused more centrally on the psychologist who treated the boy—a middle-aged, successful, but cynical professional. This so-competent man recognized that he would be able to deal with the boy, to bring him to a more rational, less passionate stance toward life. He would be able to help the boy become one of us.

But this psychologist had lost his own dreams, lived competently, but without passion, without meaning, without anything to live or die for. The central issue of the play becomes, not the motive that the young man had for his actions, but the lack of motive the psychologist had to cure him. This doctor must decide whether or not he has the right to deprive the boy of dreams, illusions, visions that give passionate focus to his life, even if the dreams are deranged and the passion destructive. At least he is alive. The doctor fears that to be well, to be "normal," may necessarily be to be bored and boring as well.

A further impression of mid-life has been dramatically imbedded in the consciousness of most Americans through the recently popular novel and movie *Ordinary People*. Again, while the central character is an adolescent searching for a direction, and meaning, a "bumper sticker" to guide his life after his brother's death, the lives of his parents are perhaps more traumatic as they face the same issues at mid-life. Conrad's mother, played so convincingly by Mary Tyler Moore (who was simultaneously experiencing her own real-life, mid-life crisis), suffers a crisis of limits regarding her entire fabricated meaning. She has built a life of middle-class, expected, predicted comforts and values—husband, home, family, golf club. Roles are reversed from the stereotypical unfeeling man and sensitive woman. Here the mother is unable to deal with her affective life, unable to face one son's death, another's mental illness, and her own inadequacy and fear. She refuses to enter into her living son's struggle, protecting herself from the kind of pain parents face when they realize they have not parented perfectly, or even well. Shattered dreams and hopes leave her crumbling, but refusing to re-examine herself, her family, her own shaky meaning systems. In a final scene, when she is unable to embrace her son, she is also unable to embrace a broken life, an imperfect world, a fragile self.

Her husband cries, becomes painfully vulnerable, puts a hope-filled arm around his son, and chooses to go on, despite the losses, into a new-birth—with its yet unseen but promised possibilities.

Every family of ordinary people deals with similar if quite distinct tragedies, wrestles with similar choices, and either dies or rises to new and better life. The popularity of *Ordinary People* speaks loudly of the universal recognition that this mother and father are all of us as we face the shattered dreams of middle years.

The field of psychology provides another fictional but too real impression of the chaotic mid-life in Judith Rossner's brilliant *August*. This novel analyzes the plight of Dr. Lulu Shinefeld, a clinical analyst, in the middle of her life. Early in the book, Rossner speaks of an associate of Lulu's in a passage that becomes partially thematic for the book:

"Leif Seaver had done pioneering work on middle-aged men and the fear of death that led them to abandon their families and begin younger, duplicate families that would allow them, as they looked around each day, to pretend that they were fifteen or twenty years younger than the mark at which reality placed them. He had written movingly of the misery of many of these men, cut off from their own histories and suffering terribly: finding themselves at social gatherings with twenty-year-olds for whom they represented, at best, a paterfamilias; jogging frantically to rid themselves of middle-aged flab; feeling embarrassed upon bumping into old friends; living often, with a continuing sense of unreality. One such patient . . . who had led an exemplary life, public and private, had, on the day he turned fifty, packed a suitcase, kissed his wife goodbye and moved to a hotel. Shortly after divorcing his wife, he had married a beautiful eighteen-year-old model and not long after that had suffered multiple fractures during a brawl at a discotheque when he tried to beat up a nineteen-year-old boy who made a pass at his new wife."[6]

Though limited in its treatment of only the upper-middle-class middle-aged, Alan Alda's delightful film *Four Seasons* poignantly presents three couples engaging in the same mid-journey joustings. The waning of sexual powers, the quest for younger women, the disillusionment of marriage after many apparently happy years, the struggle to understand children and to hold onto youth, the misplaced meaning found in material symbols like boats, expensive cars, or escapist trips away from life, the painful facing of limitations when confronted by husband, wife or friends, all humorously presented, still touch universal issues of the middle-years. While we laugh at these couples' foibles, we recognize them as our own.

Most of us, somewhere in the middle of our lives, are

forced to come to grips with our relationship with our parents. Usually we have in some sense "divorced" them earlier, achieving independence, but still they are a part of us forever. The book and movie *I Never Sang for My Father* captures this portrait of the desire to make peace with our parents, embrace them with all their faults, love them even in their inadequacy because they are a large part of what had made us the people we are. The ability to forgive our parents, to get on about our lives without blaming them for who or what we have become, frequently constitutes one of the central tasks of mid-life transition.

Finally, in this rapid, random glance at artistic impressions of mid-life, the wonderful movie *My Dinner with Andre* portrays a man who has successfully completed most of his mid-life tasks returning to tell a friend about his adventures on this journey. As they sit and talk over dinner, Andre's friend cannot understand anything that Andre talks about. He tries to respond, with pathetic ineptitude at every point. The film's genius lies in capturing conversation that never connects, talk that never communicates, a friendship that is over because one party has moved to a new place where the other is unwilling or unable to follow. This rambling, brilliant mid-life reflection will hopefully be recast one day for women. We long for a film called *My Dinner with Marie,* followed by another film in which Marie and Andre share their own hard-earned adulthood, discovering the mutual enrichment available to men and women when they have crossed to a new place and landed, more or less, on their feet.

Our impressions of mid-life and its struggles and opportunities arise not just outside us, in art or film or book, but out of our own experiences and the struggles shared with our friends. You would undoubtedly hear many of the same questions, struggles, dashed hopes, shattered dreams, longings for rebirth emerge if you were to reread the letters you have received, or were to listen in your imagination to the messages you recall from friends. Some excerpts from letters we have received will perhaps demonstrate the kind of things you too would hear.

Excerpts from a letter from a male friend, age forty-seven: After a long, personal discussion of how religion has been changing in his life, he concludes:

> So there I am; clearly I have lost my faith; what I don't know is whether in that loss I am finally finding faith. If I'm really honest, I can't call myself "Catholic," or "Christian," but I can call myself a "man," and "alive."
> . . . I'm not unhappy, depressed or frightened; I'm just terribly alone, though it is neither terrible or lonely. My being seems strange to me, and new and rather uncommunicable (obviously). Who is this me who is not me? Where should I go except into the dark? I'm neither afraid to live or die, but somehow long for both.

In a slightly later letter, after explaining why he no longer seems able to call himself "Catholic" or "Christian," the same friend writes:

> There, my friend, are my heresies. Perhaps you see more now why I have no community, feel no groups of people who are where I am. Oh, I still go to mass, still pray with them, share life with them; but always there is a terrible loneliness in the midst of their celebrating, and fellowship, and ritual security. All I seem to have left is a firm conviction that Life is, and is good; that death is an aberration to be lived through, that there are many realms of reflective life ahead, and that my entrance into these realms is through faith in love. So I am called to stand alone, and even lonely in the face of nothingness, emptiness; there I must reach out in love toward no one

known, or seen, or felt, or even believed in. And I do as
much as I am able. Really as absurd as it sounds, I am
very happy, and very much at peace. I'm not afraid. I just
feel like all the props have been knocked out, that I'm
falling into a void somehow filled with life.

Not all our friends, or yours, are as articulate as this,
but many of them will speak, if we listen carefully, of the
same isolation, the same dying of previously helpful symbol
systems, the passing away of previous understandings of
life and God. We do not want to minimize the pain of the
unique experience of this writer, recognizing himself personally cut off from others, but experiences so much like
this are far more universal than he knows. In fact, his experience of unicity and aloneness, in what seems to us to be
an almost universal struggle, is what impels us to this book
and these reflections. Each of us feels so dreadfully alone,
and in fact we are, but there is a deep, shared commonality
of passage that binds us together. We can support,
strengthen, challenge one another. What we undergo is
suffered more easily when we know we are not alone.

Another letter from a male counselee:

I don't know what to tell you. I've thought so often of
writing, of calling out for help, and always I decided just
to carry on for a while, always claiming I was too busy,
or, perhaps, too depressed. I feel that I have failed myself, failed to be who I am intended (I think) to be, too
weak to praise, to pray, to believe. I've felt like a character that Laura Nyro complains about in a song of hers,
a junkie that she's arguing with: "You've got no guts,
no gospel, and you got no brain." So it has seemed. No
guts, no gospel . . .

You helped me to see my life as sacrament, as
bread for, among others, [my wife]. But I have not suc-

ceeded at this. I have drifted, lost on some magnificent dark lake, rowing my way blindly away from God. We have found no church here [in a new city where he had moved] that feeds us adequately. . . . My own prayer life, of course, has suffered. It has dried up. I no longer know why I'm here, what I'm trying to give, how on earth I can hope to feed anyone when I don't even remember what real food tastes like.

Perhaps I am writing all of this now as a sign that the worst part is over. Perhaps I do feel myself coming back to life, somewhat, which means looking around, reflecting, staring at the sky, listening to music (really listening closely), just sitting, thinking. I find myself at odd moments thinking about something and without thought, crossing myself; a prayer, a link, brief as the life of a fly, but there. . . .

I fear that in our conversations . . . I was always in control. I'd say "I'm lost," but say it in a perfectly controlled voice. I'm too well trained, you see. I have a hard time just letting go, abandoning myself, have a hard time just saying "help." I am too accustomed to working things out by myself.

Are not this man's themes and questions, however painfully personal and individual, shared by most of us as we move into the mysterious second half of life? When we cannot find God in any of the old familiar places, God finds us with a sign, a song, a gesture, a wonder at some previously unseen beauty of our world. But we do not, cannot control the presence or this losing of control. This walking where we would rather not go echoes again and again, like an incessant refrain, if not sung then hummed softly in the deepest recesses of our mid-life minds.

The depression this man speaks of is also a common note for many men and women in middle life. A woman in her mid-forties writes us:

> I had difficulty sorting out in my mind the whys of my
> depressions . . . somehow not understanding why God
> didn't just heal me of this problem, not understanding
> why I was not surrendering sufficiently for God to heal
> me—why in hell did I have to hurt so much! And yet, I
> had not even been able to articulate these questions. I
> suppose I didn't really know what the questions were!!!

This loss of balance, confusion, uncertainty in all of life
spills over into deep-rooted faith questions. The depression
experienced leads many to search anywhere to fill the void.
In the same letter this woman articulates a common experience of this quest:

> I realize that I have been searching for that "someone"
> who would be all things to me . . . would be my security,
> my love, my future. I know I looked at you as such a
> person and have done that with others, all the time not
> understanding that God is that someone—Jesus is the
> person to be all things.

We articulate this realization much more easily than
we translate it into the fabric of our lives. We recognize
painfully that no one will ever be able to fill all our voids, and
we must "kiss sleeping beauty goodbye," forever. There is
no prince or princess to wake us from the sleep we now recognize made up much of the first half of our lives.

We discover other faith and human issues, impressions
of mid-life in an insightful letter from a woman just moving
into her forties:

> These months of therapy have been good for me. I fin-
> ished in April. Mostly I learned that I can make "free
> choices" if I really want to—about how to behave, reach,
> respond, take consequences, take responsibility, etc. I'm
> really becoming aware of how truly free I am, and how
> much responsibility I have for my choices big and small.

The area in which choice-making is most significant for me now is that of independence and solitari-
ness, vs. dependence and personal relationships. On
the one hand I yearn for independence (even complete
independence, including financial) while on the other
hand it would be so nice to experience intimacy with
someone. I'm not talking about celibacy versus a sexual
intimacy. I think I'm talking about identity and contain-
ment of self, and how to get that together with vulnerability and intimacy and the real or apparent "loss of
self" which that involves. . . .

I find myself shying away from intimacy. I don't let
any one friend get too close. . . . I have good friends but
it bothers me that I easily let long spaces of time elapse
without any direct communication. I am not willing to
be dependent on someone else for emotional support. . . . I know that if I wanted an intimate relationship, I have the capability, tools, etc. That's no problem.
It's the "not wanting" that is new and different for me.
I experience the consequences—loneliness— so that's
what makes me question myself.

There's another thing going on, I am seeing my
"shadow side" more and more everyday. I label people
so easily, and don't easily forgive. . . . It bothers me
when my efforts go unrecognized and when I am not
thanked. I am impatient with people who treat me as a
"role," etc. etc. The list goes on: VERY BIG SHADOW!

So how come I'm seeing all this yucky stuff? Part
of me is a bit disappointed . . . but another part heaves
a sigh of relief. I don't have to "work at" humility, because there is plenty of real cause. Part of the relief
comes simply from truth. How delicious is truth. I mean
this most sincerely; that taste is satisfying.

Over and over in the pages to come, these same themes
will arise: needing another to walk with us (hence, for her,

a therapist, but it could as well be a friend, a spouse, a spiritual director); struggling to balance autonomy and intimacy, aloneness and closeness; accepting what are the least admirable parts of ourselves.

Finally, in this taste of personal stories shared with us, some words from a woman who responded to us in a class we taught on mid-life spirituality. This woman was giving her personal response to our reading of the above letters:

> The pain is that I cannot easily know God. Sometimes I look beside me and see that he has been there all along. But when I cannot find him I am desolate and I say that he does not exist. It's still the same, but if I say that he doesn't exist, at least *I've said it* and not God. Comfort me, comfort me!
>
> When he is within me, he transfuses my being. It cannot be described.
>
> The absence of God is also the Presence of God. As I write that, the joy leaps up inside me. Soon I'll be able to bring that together!

With these reflections from friends, another word seems appropriate from a friend known only through his searching, honest books, always tinged with enough humor to capture the human condition. Sam Keen, in *To a Dancing God,* speaks of his own mid-life experience:

> It was as if my interior space had been hollowed out, and boredom, anxiety, despair, impotence, erratic wilfulness, and shameful self-consciousness were dumped in and agitated like clothes in a washer. These demons whirled around my inner emptiness, their harsh screams reverberating and blending into painful cacophony in the vacuum. I was possessed by vertigo. No way to stop the swirl. No solid ground. No place to rest. No power to discover or cling to what was satisfying.[7]

A variety of voices, variety of experiences—but all speak in one fashion or another of a death to what has been and a possible rebirth to something new, infinitely better, certainly different. Can we bring these impressions together? That will be the task of this book, but here we can offer a summary, perhaps best placed within the context of spirituality.

We have said in another book that:

SPIRITUALITY IS
THE STYLE OF A PERSON'S RESPONSE TO CHRIST,
BEFORE THE CHALLENGES OF EVERYDAY LIFE,
IN A GIVEN HISTORICAL AND CULTURAL MOMENT.[8]

In the middle of our lives, the "challenges of everyday life" have some generally shared particularities, touched upon, hinted at, presumed by writers, poets, film makers, and folks like ourselves and our friends. We summarize them now in no particular order of importance or universality.

CHALLENGES AT MID-LIFE

1. *General disillusionment:* Whatever seemed to form a basis for our life no longer does; religious symbols, psychological certainty, a particular lifestyle no longer seem adequate to the realities of life.
2. *Crisis of feelings:* We cannot feel, or we feel too much. But, whichever, we are not at home any longer with our affective life; like many other things, our feelings seem out of control.
3. *Resistance to stereotypical roles:* In every area of our lives we are no longer comfortable as "the wife of . . ."

or "Sister," or "Father," or whatever title has previously managed to encompass our being rather well.

4. *Sense of failure:* Subjectively, whatever we have tried we have not been good enough—at parenting, or praying, or writing, or, especially, at loving. Ironically, others often view us as eminently successful.

5. *Anxiety and guilt:* As we become aware of our failures in the past, our inadequacy now, and our uncertainty about the future . . . not only do we recognize that we have failed, but also that it is our fault, and we are unsure, left to our own devices, how to change this sad reality.

6. *Sense of loneliness:* Our struggles are our own, unique, unspeakable, unshared, and we grapple with a sense of being so definitely other-than everyone we have known, or even ourselves as we have known that self.

7. *Feelings of burn-out, or breakdown:* "I can't keep on, can't do *it,*" whatever *it* may be, anymore. My meaning system is defunct, my relationships exhausting, my energy sapped.

8. *Last chance mentality:* Especially sexually, but often in other parts of life as well, I need to do it *now* or sooner, or I never will; life is slipping away.

9. *Disconnectedness:* From ourselves, others, and especially from God. Whatever had worked before in prayer or life to help make connections seems inadequate now.

10. *Depression:* In various degrees, and varied intensity, but always somewhat there . . . like the sadness at death, the death of ourselves, or parts of that self that we had known, and, if not loved, at least depended on.

11. *Journey, vocation change, job adjustment:* How often in mid-life, consciously or not, we make a move, trying

to find something, but always bringing ourselves with us, and though we go out to discover some new life, some prince or principle of peace, even if we find it, we are tempted to try to go home again.

12. *Concern (perhaps obsession) with the past:* A growing and continuing desire to understand where we have come from, our family, our religious roots, our nature and nurturing, consciously or unconsciously needing to know why we are as we are.

13. *A move toward interiority:* Seeking, even desperately, a solitude we have perhaps previously run from, heightening our reflective awareness, and, again, constantly asking "why?"

These thirteen, apparently unlucky hallmarks of the mid-life condition can perhaps be seen more simply by suggesting that:

Our central pervasive issue is the loss of youth.
Our central faith issue is a sense of brokenness.
Our central psychological issue is the demise of our myth about ourselves.

We are invited in the middle of the stream of life to deal with the unfinished business of the past, to cope with the physical changes that assail us. We are aware as never before of issues of affectivity, intimacy, sexuality that need to be settled. We are equally aware of a growing sense of our mortality—we and all whom we love will die, in fact are dying. We wonder how to sustain faith when God seems absent or perhaps is no longer imaged as benign, when most sensible consolation is absent, and especially when we seek it through prayer, or ritual, or any personal effort. We wonder who we are and what we are worth. And all of this goes on at more or less the same moment.

Spirituality seems to us, in general and preliminary terms, the invitation to respond somehow to Christ in faith before the challenges of everyday life.

Before we go on, or you, our readers, do, we invite you to close this book and pause: listen to your heart. Are these experiences, struggles, opportunities yours? Do any of these people sound like you, or part of you, or anyone you know? Have we given you some impression of the reality you know in your deepest heart, your guts? If this experience seems in any way a shared one, we can justifiably move to a more systematic look at the same experience through the eyes of those who from various angles have studied human development at mid-life.

Notes

1. T.S. Eliot, "The Love Song of J. Alfred Prufrock," *The Complete Poems and Plays, 1909–1950* (New York, Harcourt, Brace, and World, Inc., 1952) pp.3–7.

2. T.S. Eliot, "The Journey of the Magi," *op. cit.*, pp. 68–69.

3. Kathleen Raine, "Northumbrian Sequence IV," *The Collected Poems* (New York: Random House, 1956) pp. 115–117.

4. May Sarton, *Selected Poems* (New York, W.W. Norton & Co., 1978) p. 88.

5. Ingmar Bergman, *The Marriage Scenarios* (New York, Pantheon Books, 1978) p. 211.

6. Judith Rossner, *August* (New York, Warner Books, 1984) p. 51.

7. Sam Keene, *To a Dancing God* (New York, Harper and Row, 1970) p. 131.

8. L. Patrick Carroll and Katherine Marie Dyckman, *Inviting the Mystic and Supporting the Prophet* (New York, Paulist Press, 1981) p. 79.

2

The Overarching Model:
The Mid-Life Challenge of Carl Jung

The onset of the psychospiritual tasks of the middle of life have been called many things: mid-life crisis, second journey, crisis of limits, dark night, second adolescence, experience of nothingness, the void. Whatever the terminology, the experiential reality is very much the same. Mid-life is an invitation, perhaps a mandate to creation, to become what God calls us to be.

Traditional spiritual classics have presented the experience as primarily a challenge of faith. This "second journey" is essential for human development as well. The two are inseparable. Clement of Alexandria remarked somewhere that the one who knows self knows God. The experience of oneself is prerequisite to, or at least concurrent with, the experience of God.

The past twenty-five to thirty years have witnessed a fruitful partnership between depth psychology and ascetical or mystical theology. The richness of mystics like John of the Cross, Teresa of Avila, Meister Eckhart, Julian of Norwich, the author of *The Cloud of Unknowing*, as well as the more contemporary Thomas Merton, has been enhanced and affirmed by such great figures in the field of social science as C.G. Jung, Erik Erikson, Karen Horney, Abraham Maslow and James Fowler. We will touch on the work of many of these in subsequent chapters. Here, as a first and overarching model, we will look at the thought of Carl Jung.

Jung offers us a model of adult developmental psychology that is highly compatible with past and current religious thinking. Though originally a disciple of Freud, Jung broke with him in 1913, largely over their different understanding of the unconscious. Jung was thirty-seven at the time and moving into confrontation with his own inner life. To facilitate this inner journey, Jung resigned his professorship at the University of Zurich and his presidency of the International Congress of Psychoanalysis.

Jung's profound personal experience at mid-life coupled with extensive research and a broad practice as a psychiatrist gave rise to a scheme of the human life cycle, perceived in two central phases.

The first half of life, incorporating childhood and youth, is essentially a period of ego development, or growth in consciousness. The ego is the center of the conscious personality. It is the "I" part of us with which we identify, the part that does the willing and choosing in life. The process of ego development moves from an unconscious condition in which the individual is in a state of primal unity with all the polarities contained within to a sense of subjective self ("I-ness"), and thus to an awareness of interior and exterior tensions which greater consciousness brings. Essentially the ego develops as the product of others' expectations—parents, teachers, church, peers, etc. The ego is largely made in the image and likeness of society as the young person takes up, in one form or another, the collective consciousness of the community of which he or she is part.

This first half of life is characterized by a movement *outward* as an individual learns to adapt and accommodate to exterior reality. The individual develops an awareness and relatability to others and the world in ever broadening concentric circles.

Jung perceives the ego, the controller of this conscious

life, as the center of the conscious personality, but not as the supreme force. The Self incorporates and is the center of the total personality, both conscious and unconscious. The ego is subordinate to the Self and is related to it like a part of the whole. However, during this first stage of life, the ego tends to perceive itself as the supreme force of the personality.

In puberty, what Jung calls the "second or psychic birth," greater consciousness emerges. With the eruption of the sexual potential, a conscious differentiation from parents occurs and a protective psychic ambience which allowed for earlier ego development recedes. Individual consciousness pushes away from the confining dock of parental ideals, values, norms and begins to swim on its own. This latter stage of development maintains until the mid-life transition, somewhere in the thirties (or forties, or fifties, if at all). Jung maintains that not everyone makes the transition to this second half of life, speaking of those who escape or avoid the transition as "hypochondriacs, niggards, doctrinaires, applauders of the past or eternal adolescents."[1]

As we continue our consideration of the first half of life, other elements are significant. One of the tasks of this primary ego development consists in establishing what Jung calls a *persona*, a sort of public image or mask by which one relates to the outer world, the outward face of the psyche or personality. (Originally the word *persona* referred to the mask worn by an actor or actress to portray a specific role.) In our experience, we know that we and others have differing images, or faces, for different parts of our life—one professional image, another at home by ourselves or with friends. There are days when all of us feel particularly out of sorts or vulnerable. It is not to our advantage to let these feelings be seen by everyone. The use of our *persona*, then, is a necessary part of the ego's ability to cope with life. The world would be a jarring place indeed if only raw psyches, unaccommodated to situations and persons, were presented to the world. People who neglect the development of a *persona* tend to offend others and have difficulty establishing themselves in the world.

On the other hand, our *persona* can be largely a composite of the expectations of others so that we do not have a real sense of who we are; we become only a collection of the masks that others want, simply living a "role," or a series of roles. We are all familiar with the dynamic business man or woman who cannot be otherwise at home; the super-mom who has no time for herself; the doctor or priest who is uneasy unless there is someone to heal or counsel. The role has taken over and there is no sense of identity beneath it, or apart from it. Like Jenny, the psychiatrist in Ingmar Bergman's film *Face to Face*: "We act the play. We learn our lines. We know what people want us to say. We lie. In the end, it's not even deliberate."[2]

While the *persona* is necessary for survival, we risk becoming too identified with our own or others' expectations of who we are. Our conformity or accommodation needs to be conscious and chosen. It would be wonderful to live without hypocrisy or deception, but in reality we need to adapt and accommodate and so we choose to do so. At any rate, the painful breakdown of one's *persona*, the inability to carry off the public image, is one of the signals of the onset of the second half of the life-cycle which calls for a full flowering of the authentic personality.

The individual is called to undergo a third and decisive birth, a refashioning of the authentic self into the image and likeness of God. Jung sees the crisis of mid-life as a shifting of the center of gravity in the personality from the ego to the Self, the authentic center of the personality, and a redirection of psychic energy from the outer to the inner world:

"For a young person it is almost a sin, at least a danger, to be too preoccupied with oneself; but for the aging person it is a duty and a necessity to devote serious attention to oneself."³

If *accommodation* to others and the world was important in the first half of life, then *individuation*, or the process by which we become our true self, is the key word for the second. As certain poles of the personality are developed in consciousness, their opposites in the unconscious become energized and seek expression in the personality. The emerging intensity of the unconscious disrupts the order of conscious life. That is why it seems that just as we are beginning to get everything together, the bottom drops out of our existence.

Individuation's dynamic and often painful process differentiates various facets of our inner world in the personal and collective layers of the unconscious that make up the total personality. Paul's "hidden self" (Eph 3:14) begins to reveal itself.

Let us briefly recount a friend's dream, a typical midlife dream, that illustrates the instinctive inner forces of the unconscious that need to be recognized and brought to consciousness at mid-life:

> I am standing on the front porch of a house, alongside of which runs a lovely stream [water is a common symbol for the unconscious]. Fascinated by the stream I move [away from her house where she is "at home"] closer, only to see bright, exotic flowers growing beneath the water. Surprised and delighted, I put one foot on a rock in the stream bed to steady myself [the search is precarious]. As I bend to get a better look, I am immediately aware of a large, thick snake beneath the porch, ready to strike if I make any further advances.

There is a dark part of herself lurking there, demanding attention if she is to capture the beauty beneath the water's surface.

At this point it may help to introduce a graphic representation of Jung's understanding of the personality, adapted from the work of Josef Goldbrunner.[4] Consider the graph's upper half for a pictorial presentation of what we have discussed so far about Jung's understanding of the first half of life. The task of the second half is seen as involving, to a much greater degree, the facets of the psyche indicated in the bottom half of the circle.

Jung distinguishes three levels of psychic development: (1) consciousness, (2) the personal unconscious, and (3) the collective unconscious. As we have indicated, the ego controls conscious life.

The personal unconscious consists of repressed material (not acceptable to the ego ideal), forgotten contents or contents whose intensity was not strong enough to reach consciousness. This personal unconscious also contains constellations of energy called complexes, sub-personalities within the psyche which can be triggered by a remark or action of another, e.g., inferiority or mother complex. This level of unconscious is as far as Freud went. Freudian psychoanalysis was seen as a means of siphoning off repressed material, and raising it to the level of consciousness in order to be dealt with. In more simple terms, Freud's understanding involved getting all the "junk" out of the unconscious into the light of day. For Freud, the distasteful contents of this unconscious were largely placed there before the age of six. For Jung there is much of worth in the unconscious and it is drawn from the experiences of all of life, as well as the composite experiences of all people even before our birth.

For Jung, it is also within this level of the personal unconscious that we meet a generally neglected figure, the

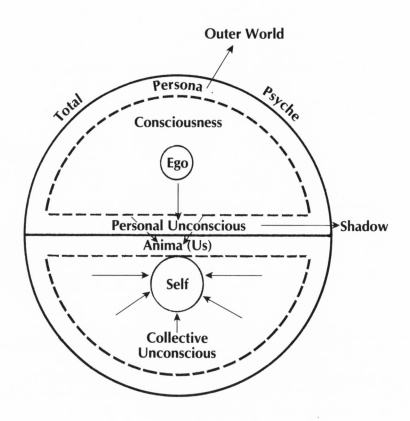

Outer World

Total

Persona

Psyche

Consciousness

Ego

Personal Unconscious

Shadow

Anima (Us)

Self

Collective
Unconscious

shadow—a term used for the negative side of the personality. This shadow can be seen as the personification of evil tendencies within (anger, lust, greed) which we would prefer not to acknowledge, or apparent weaknesses with which we would rather not deal (lack of courage, sexuality, an inability to assert ourself). The one who pays attention to the shadow may discover much that is pure gold. As Rollo May remarked, we must take care not to lose our devils or we may lose our angels too. Although underdeveloped, the *shadow* promises great possibilities for growth and development of the full personality of one who recognizes and owns this dark side. In recognizing what seems unwanted by the ego, we discover deeper parts of ourselves, and an energy that counters the imbalance of an early developed ego. We need, for example, to recognize our lack of assertiveness so that we can become confident and assured. We need to recognize aspects of sexuality so that we can draw power from that energy to fully love. We need to know, name, and embrace our anger lest we remain passive-aggressive in our relationships with those who are different from ourselves.

Jung suggests several means to draw out this *shadow* into consciousness. The most significant tool we possess is an attentive listening to our dreams in which what we have buried in our unconscious life bubbles to the surface. We can also notice those things that bother us about another human being because usually that is a "projection" of what we do not like about ourselves. Finally, those things that especially strike our funny-bone indicate the incongruity our unconscious senses in relationship to our more conscious life.

The *persona* unacquainted with the *shadow* side is dangerous to self and others, for he or she is at the mercy of repressed, despised desires and emotions. Such a person tends to be humorless, judgmental, and proficient at pro-jecting onto others what he or she is unaware of in self. One cannot advance in the mid-life journey until he or she has dealt with the *shadow*.

In the first book of her Earthsea trilogy, *A Wizard of Earthsea*, Ursula Le Guin deals with resistance to the shadow, and the wonderful possibilities that are part of own-ing and claiming it. Ged, the main character (who is each of us), flees a hideous creature, but realizes in great fear that he must face it. In that awe-ful encounter both the shadow and Ged speak the same word, his name:

> ... Ged had neither lost nor won, but naming the shadow of his death with his own name, had made him-self whole: a man: who knowing his whole true self, cannot be used or possessed by any power other than himself, and whose life therefore is lived for life's sake and never in the service of ruin, or pain, or hatred, or the dark. In the *Creation of Ea*, which is the oldest song, it is said, "Only in silence the word, only in dark the light, only in dying life; bright the hawk's flight on the empty sky."[5]

Psychologists had been studying consciousness since the 1860's, but Freud was the first to initiate study of the unconscious. For Freud, the unconscious corresponds roughly with what Jung called, more specifically, the *personal* unconscious. The concept of the *collective* uncon-scious most singularly distinguishes Jung's work from Freud. This collective unconscious differs from personal unconscious because it does not depend on our personal history or experience for its existence. The contents of the collective unconscious are rooted in the history and expe-rience of all humankind. We inherit its deposit from com-mon experience. Just as our bodies are linked through the evolutionary process, so too are our psyches. This still-disputed realization constituted a landmark assertion in the history of psychology.

Jung's suspicions about the existence of this collective unconscious were initially confirmed by an experience of his in 1906.[6] He had a chance encounter with a minimally educated young man about thirty who was suffering from a paranoid form of schizophrenia. The young man asked Jung to squint his eyes and look at the sun in order to see penises dancing in the solar wind. Jung listened carefully to him, and for some unknown reason recorded his exact words. Four years later Jung came across a recently edited papyrus thought to contain a liturgy of an obscure Mithraic cult. This papyrus presented a description of the sun with penises dancing in the solar wind, almost word for word the vision of the young man in the hospital. It was impossible for this patient to have had access to this esoteric description. In his schizophrenia, something bonded him with a collective unconscious deep in the shared human psyche. Jung found further evidence for this collective unconscious in the commonality of themes in patients' dreams, in fairytales, ancient myths and fables.

Within this realm of the collective unconscious reside what Jung called archetypes, elemental or primordial images established over thousands of generations of human development. These images, similar to ordinary negatives which need to be developed, are like pre-dispositions or potential for further development rather than passed-on, specific memories. "To say that something is an archetype means it is an essential building block of the personality. Or, to use the word in its adjective form, to say that something is 'archetypal' means that it is 'typical' for all human beings."[7] Typical experiences and motifs in life take on a certain luminosity or being within each individual's own

conscious experience—that is, the general archetype as-
sumes a particularity in the life of an individual; thus, earth-
mother, God, death, rebirth, the hero, the wise old woman
or man, the child, are examples of archetypes specified in
the unconscious of each individual out of his or her particular (conscious) experience. The archetype cannot be
known in itself, but only through one's life experiences.

> There are as many archetypes as there are typical sit-
> uations in life. Endless repetition has engraved these
> experiences into our psychic constitution, not in the
> form of images filled with content, but at first only in
> forms without content, representing merely the possi-
> bility of a certain type of perception and action.[8]

The *persona* and the *shadow*, of which we have already
spoken, are archetypes. If the persona is the "outward face
of the psyche," the face we present to the world, the inward
face is the archetype called either *anima* (woman within)
for men, or the *animus* (man within) for women. If the masculine dominates in the conscious personality, the feminine
will act as its opposite pole in the inner personality, and vice
versa. The *anima* and *animus*, representing two modes of
consciousness or perception, constitute the means by
which we relate to the inner world. They form (individually)
a bridge between the ego and the world of unconsciousness.
The *animus(a)* functions to filter the contents of the collective unconscious through to the conscious mind. (It may
help to refer to the Jungian chart to see this schematically
presented.) The individuation process (or the task of mid-
life) calls for a delicate balance between opening oneself to
the contents of the unconscious while at the same time remaining rooted in consciousness so that these contents can

be gradually integrated into the conscious personality. Hence the need for the mid-life person, wrestling with this precarious process, to remain "balanced" by way of friends, family, spiritual director, worshiping community, etc.

As with all the elements of the unconscious, the *animus* and *anima* have both positive and negative aspects. What woman is not familiar with that inner voice that tells her she cannot do what she desires, that she will fail, is not good enough, strong enough, etc. (the negative animus). What man has not heard the insinuations of a witch-like carping inner figure constantly hassling him, telling him "that's not it at all!" (the negative anima). We need to make friends with these inner voices, *animus* or *anima*, to be straightforward and firm in honestly seeking guidance in developing these neglected parts of our personality.

Irene de Castillejo suggests that it is helpful to name and give personality to the various parts of the *animus* for it is a multifaceted reality:

> In trying to contact the *animus* we tend to think of him as one person, although we know he has a multitude of shapes. He can appear as an old man or as a little boy, a learned scholar or an aviator, a god or a devil, a romantic lover or the prosaic figure who styles himself one's husband. . . . Now, if only we can succeed in splitting the animus up into distinct and separate persons, we can deal with him. Then I can kneel and ask a blessing of the priest, befriend the feeble minded boy, face firmly, but with due respect, the devil and order the mealy-mouthed sycophant out of my house. But woe betide me if I lump them all together, call it the *animus*, and try to deal with that.[9]

For the man, the *anima*, likewise, presents a diversity of faces to the dreamer: the critical older woman, the cool, pale blond, the aging prostitute, the peasant woman, the young, seductive girl.

> Since men do live psychologically in a harem, it is useful to get to know one's inner household. We do well to know by what fascination we are bewitched, turned into phallic animal, petrified into immobility, or lured underwater and away from real life. We do well to know whom we are unconsciously following in counsel, where our Cinderella sits in dirt and ashes or Snow White lies in poisoned sleep, what hysterical feminine tricks we play deceivingly on ourselves with affects and moods, which Muse inspires or Beatrice ignites and which is the true favorite who moves the deepest possibilities of our nature and holds our fate.[10]

When the *animus(a)* is not recognized, it becomes projected onto persons of the opposite sex and we make another the embodiment of behavior, desires, characteristics that we have denied in ourselves. Thus, the other can become the object of a false and impossible projection of all our hopes and needs. The experience of "falling in love" often involves such a projection as we seek to find in another those characteristics we have not, or cannot find in ourselves. We hope, dream, expect the other to fulfill what is lacking in us. The balance that can come in mid-life invites us to internalize and embrace the archetype of the opposite sex (that is, *anima* for men, *animus* for women) so as to become integrated and whole in expressing all the qualities of mature development.

The archetype of wholeness is the Self, the organizing principle of the personality. This Self is the central archetype in the collective unconscious, uniting the personality and giving it a sense of oneness and integration. The Self acts as a kind of magnet, drawing together all opposing elements or polarities in the psyche or personality: consciousness and unconsciousness, death and resurrection, masculine and feminine, feeling and thinking, body and spirit, the individual psyche and the collective psyche. (Though Jung himself does not explicitly equate the Self with God, he certainly intimates that it is in the discovery of Self that we discover our union with God and all that is God's.)

After this lengthy, but still all-too-cursory description of the language, thought, and categories of Jung, we want to indicate, out of his analysis, what creates the pain and the tension, the disorientation so often experienced in the middle of our lives.

The task in the first half of life, as we have said, is to develop a strong ego, a firm center of conscious life. At midlife, the center of gravity of the personality shifts from the ego to the Self. For the ego, it is not unlike people's reaction to the Copernican discovery that the earth revolves around the sun and not vice versa—a total transference of belief and expectation. The ego which had been firmly in control is at a loss. Just when the conscious personality had begun to "get it together," everything begins to fall apart. Up to this point, the ego had perceived itself as a kind of god; it thought it *was* the Self. Further, the ego finds itself hammered by the demands of the outer world—which are reflected in consciousness—and the needs of the inner world—which emerge in long-forgotten, or newly awakened feelings and desires, dreams, fantasies, longings, and projections. The ego has a feeling of defeat and behaves all the more defensively, defiantly, self-righteously, and thus sets up a vicious circle which only increases its feelings of inferiority and disorientation.

> When the pull of opposites appears, the psyche is demanding wholeness. The ego's tendency, however, is to

solve the problem of the opposites and of the psychic tension they create by accepting one side (and identifying with it) and rejecting the other (and repressing it). This produces a conflict between the Self, which is made up of opposites and desires their "marriage," and the ego, which hates tension and seeks security and comfort through defense, one-sidedness, and identification. So the key task in this phase, when the opposites are pulling for the ego's allegiance with equal urgency and conviction, is to place the ego in the service of the Self, to ask it to endure the stress of a psychological alchemy that is trying to unite the opposites in an amalgam that will also be a totally new element—psychological "gold!" This gold . . . is the conscious presence of the Self within the everyday world of egoic existence.[11]

The Self is a threat to the ego's secure existence. It demands a terrible letting-go on the part of the ego to surrender to the Self, which is, finally, the Self-for-God. Then ego illusions give way to truth and the ego is freed from having to worship itself. Generally this happens only when the person is driven by pain and frustration to exclaim, in words or in the whole of one's being: "I can't do it!" It is the "I" of the ego finally capitulating to the reality of the emerging authentic personality.

Individuation consists not in choosing conscious life or unconscious life, but in integrating the two, bringing the unconscious into consciousness by an ego-Self union that reconciles opposites and unites all opposing trends in the personality.

At mid-life, the psyche or personality seeks equilibrium, but we are tempted to collapse the tensions or polarities in either of two ways: We can regress, withdraw from the struggle, and go back to ego control, hoping to be content with an underdeveloped personality in which ego continues to identify with the Self. A hint at this inflated Ego stance occurs in extremes of attitude like taking too much blame, or too much credit for one's life: "I did it!"

The other polarity replaces ego control with control by the unconscious. Psychosis is the extreme form of this. It is not unusual, however, for a person in mid-life transition to evince signs which can also be associated with breakdown and a loss of the filters that keep an outer and an inner world significant but separate. We need to continue to tell the one from the other, but cannot ignore either. The entrance of the unconscious onto the stage of personality needs to be accomplished, but accomplished with care and recognition of the conscious, outer life as well. The balance is not easily achieved.

We want to complete this treatment of the overarching model of Carl Jung with a mid-life dream, a vivid experience of the unconscious working its way into consciousness, an exposé of archetypes that you can ponder, try to understand, and perhaps identify with: a woman's dream, filled with *animus* figures, the possibility of new birth (Self), implying both great struggle and great hope in the journey inward.

> An old woman gave me a baby . . . said I was going on a journey and that I must keep the baby alive. The old woman had animal skin clothing, wrinkled face, white hair, and walked with a stick. I took the baby . . . came to realize that I was not alone . . . a younger boy and an older man were with me. We journeyed in very cold weather. The old woman didn't come because she didn't think she'd make it.
>
> We packed the baby in ice packs to keep it alive. Even the young boy was also packed at one time in water and a plastic or ice mold. It was cold. At one point we were sitting by the fire. . . . We had to keep the baby alive.

We finally arrived at someone's home. . . . All was
well and the baby was alive, and I nursed it.

We will return to and refer to the language and thought
of Carl Jung often as we go along, for it provides the single
most comprehensive psychological schema or model to help
us know and name our mid-life experiences.

Notes

1. C.G. Jung, "The Stages of Life," in Collected Works, translated by R.F.C. Hull, Vol. 8 (Princeton, N.J.: Princeton University
Press, 1969) Par. 785, p. 399.
2. Ingmar Bergman, The Marriage Scenarios (New York:
Pantheon Books, 1978) p. 306.
3. Jung, ibid, Par. 785, p. 399.
4. Josef Goldbrunner, Individuation: A Study of the Depth
Psychology of C.J. Jung (New York: Pantheon, 1956) p. 124.
5. Ursula Le Guin, A Wizard of Earthsea (New York: Bantam
Books, 1977) pp. 180–81.
6. Jung, "The Concept of the Collective Unconscious," CW,
Vol. 9i, Par. 104–110, pp. 50–52.
7. John Sanford, Evil: The Shadow Side of Reality (New York:
Crossroad, 1982) pp. 64ff.
8. Jung, Vol. 9i, Par. 99, p. 48.
9. de Castillejo, Knowing Woman (New York: Harper & Row,
1973) pp. 74–75.
10. James Hillman, Insearch (Dallas, Texas: Spring Publications, 1967) p. 101.
11. Murray Stein, In Midlife (Dallas, Texas: Spring Publications, 1983) pp. 138–39.

3

Redoing the Apparently Done:
Reflections on Erik Erikson's Developmental
Theory

Another principal contributor to the study of the total span of life is Erik Erikson, a psychoanalyst trained in the Freudian school. Like Jung, Erikson broke from Freud's circle, but his issue was more specifically Freud's emphasis on early childhood. Like Jung, Erikson perceived development occurring throughout all of human life, not just in childhood and adolescence. However, while Jung focused primarily on what we have called the mid-life transition, Erikson's research dealt with total life ego-development.

The seventh stage of Erikson's developmental schema, *generativity vs. stagnation,* roughly corresponds to Jung's mid-life transition, the struggle of ego with Self that we described in the previous section.

In his *Childhood and Society,* Erikson suggests eight stages of development in the human life-cycle. Each stage presents a specific challenge that the developing ego must meet.[1]

His first five stages encompass childhood development. Each is viewed in terms of a "virtue" ("ego-strength") overcoming a weakening tendency to which we are particularly inclined in each stage:

1- Trust vs. mistrust (c. birth to 2 years)
2- Autonomy vs. shame/doubt (c. 2–3 years)
3- Initiative vs. guilt (c. 4–5 years)
4- Industry vs. inferiority (c. 6–11 years)

45

5- Identity vs. identity confusion (c. 12–20 years)
Erikson's final three stages deal with adulthood:

6- Intimacy vs. self-absorption/isolation (young adulthood)

7- Generativity vs. stagnation (middle-age)

8- Integrity vs. despair (mature age)

As we indicated, each stage of life has its own unique struggle or developmental necessity. Erikson maintains that there are definable periods during human development in which a variety of forces (social, physical, intellectual, emotional, spiritual) interact in such a way as to become a catalyst for psychological growth into the next stage.

For example, everything in adolescence forces us to try to discover our identity, i.e., who we are apart from who parents, school, church or peer group tell us we are. Our personal identity can be discovered for the first time.

Erikson is the first developmental psychologist to use the word "crisis" to describe the struggle at each juncture in development. The crisis of each stage is an opportunity of "judgment" time, presenting a particular task to be accomplished in the process of psycho-social growth. Each crisis, therefore, provides both a period of increased vulnerability and heightened potential.

We cannot simplistically conclude that the specific task of each stage is resolved once and for all. Each will reappear in subsequent stages at a deeper, more challenging level. Thus, every major transition in our life (graduate school, new job, marriage, divorce, death of a parent, etc.) calls for a relearning of who we are, our *identity*, even though it has, to one extent or another, previously been achieved.

To relate our discussion of Erikson to our previous treatment of Carl Jung, is to provide another way of understanding the trauma and turmoil of mid-life. What Jung describes as the task of the first half of life, the establishing of a strong and independent ego, corresponds to Erikson's first six stages. The ego achieving this independence strives actively, through successive stages, for *trust, autonomy, initiative, industry, identity and intimacy.* But the amazing and painful thing is that when one reaches Erikson's seventh stage, *generativity vs. stagnation,* all of the stages must be dealt with and *all at once!*

Previous tasks had been done in an outer world under control of the ego; now at mid-life, the same tasks must be done in an *inner* relationship with the Self which we would see ultimately as the presence of the God-within.

In Jung's second half of life, the movement inward occurs as the ego becomes much more passive. It no longer initiates this growth in its own development, but becomes the recipient of the action of the Self which had ultimately been the directing force all along. Thus, this newly emerging personality must redo all its previous tasks in a different "key." This awareness helps us to understand, from another vantage point, the pain and tension experienced at mid-life, for it provides another language for the struggle between ego-consciousness and the emerging unconscious. The ego thought it had already done the job. It had learned to *trust* parents, teachers, friends, the world. With the Self now taking control the task of trust reasserts itself, but now the emerging personality must learn to trust the action of the Self, the God-within.

The ego, having achieved *autonomy,* has taken control in the outer world, learning to fend for itself. Now the Self seeks its rightful prominence, leaving consciousness panicky in its lack of control and sense of doubt. Earlier goals and expectations are demythologized. We hear so often the mid-life person's confused lament, "I can't do it," as control is painfully relinquished.

The second half of life calls for the Self's *initiative*, a deflating factor in light of the initiative previously exerted by the ego as the center of conscious life. Now confronted by my shadow side, I experience feelings of both guilt and confusion. I am forced to renegotiate previously held values and beliefs.

Industry, the pride and confidence the ego experienced in knowing how to do things well, becomes elusive and hidden. Work done in the unconscious leaves the ego feeling impotent and inferior. The feeling that I seem to have nothing to offer God or others strongly challenges my sense of worth.

The emerging *identity* of the authentic personality initially causes role confusion. "I" (the ego) no longer know who I am, deep inside. "Do I want to be who I am, or have been?" "Do I want to do what I have been doing?" This painful time of questioning leads to a re-evaluation of life's choices of marriage, priesthood, single-life, religious community, or career.

New-found *intimacy* with the Self in the darkness of faith also leaves the "I" feeling alienated from others and God. Attempts to hang on to former ways of relating in society or in prayer lead only to frustration. I am tempted to retreat from others out of fear of rejection.

The specific crisis of this time of middle life, *generativity vs. stagnation,* arises out of a realization of my own mortality, "I am no longer young." As the ultimate source of satisfaction or identity, I can now cling possessively to what I have given birth to or accomplished in the past (creating not just children, but ideas, movements, institutions, causes, art, etc.), or I can respond to the interior challenge to let go and use my power in radically new ways on behalf of others. I can stay where I am, remembering and savoring the past, indulging in a kind of unhealthy narcissism ("hypochondriacs, niggards, doctrinaires, applauders of the past or eternal adolescents . . ."), or I can risk moving into life in deeper, more interior, more creative and caring ways.

In Erikson's eighth and final stage, *integrity vs. despair,* the crisis involves a critical evaluation of my past, my actions, values, relationships, decisions, in order to arrive at full interior and exterior integrity. This too becomes a task even at mid-life.

This very sketchy outline of Erikson's stages is offered simply to indicate that the task of mid-life transition in Erikson's seventh stage involves all the stages in a painful tug of war that leaves the ego battered and confused.

The frustration and doubt that many experience in mid-life can be understood from yet another perspective. How painful it obviously is to be forced to accomplish again, now in an inner world and in relationship to the Self, what had already apparently been done, but only in a more outer, conscious way.

Note

1. Erik Erikson, *Childhood and Society* (New York: W. W. Norton, 1950). The material of this section is taken from this book in summary form with no effort to attribute each item.

4

Cautions of Carol Gilligan

Carol Gilligan, a colleague of Lawrence Kohlberg at Harvard, challenges Erik Erikson's eight stage schema for human development in her book *In a Different Voice*. She points out, as others have, that Erikson draws his conclusions from an all-male sampling. She notes that for Erikson, following the anchoring of trust by way of relationship in the first stage of infancy, all movement until stage six (intimacy) is toward autonomy and independence as *the* sign of growth. Adult intimacy (stage six) is achieved only after a sense of identity is reached. Separation, then, becomes the model and norm of development. Gilligan asserts that this is a blatantly male standard.

Quite differently, women develop identity precisely *in relationship* with others, that is, by way of intimacy.

> While for men, identity precedes intimacy and generativity in the optimal cycle of human separation and attachment, for women, these tasks seem instead to be fused. Intimacy goes along with identity, as the female comes to know herself as she is known, through her relationships with others.[1]

Thus, though Erikson's schema presents *separation* as the vehicle of development, Gilligan maintains that women's developmental experience is by way of *attachment*. This recognition of quite different norms of human development is essential not just to Gilligan but to all of us.

Moving beyond Erikson's schema, Gilligan also cri-

50

tiques Kohlberg's theory of moral development, likewise based on a totally male sampling. Once again, a woman's moral sense is closely related to her psychosocial development. Women tend to construct a moral problem as a question of care and responsibility in relationship, rather than the more "male" tendency to focus on objective rights and the ordering of theoretical principles.

> The basic image here [in Kohlberg's notion of moral maturity] is one of detachment from distorting values and relations and of trying to overcome the biases of personal involvement. In this logic, the way toward moral maturity leads in the direction of a kind of distinterestedness, an overcoming or offsetting of the biases of one's own interests and values.[2]

This recapitulates the same theme of the proper vehicle for human development: separation or attachment.

As Gilligan points out, development of moral thinking in a woman involves changes in understanding of "responsibility" and "relationship" rather than further acquisition of formal logic. The logic underlying women's "ethic of care" is a psychological logic of relationship rather than a formal logic of hierarchical principles. What has often been derided as "woman's logic" is neither irrational nor an underdeveloped form of thought; rather, it has clear logic and rationality and is closely and specifically in touch with reality. For the woman, moral dilemmas are seen predominantly in terms of relationships and conflicting responsibilities rather than the application of universal principles. Carol Gilligan proposes three aspects of moral development particularly significant at middle life for women. Each perspective (she resists the word "stages") represents a more complex understanding of the relationship between "self" and "other," while each transition reflects a critical reinterpretation of the meaning of "selfish" and "responsible."[3]

Perspectives:

(1) Caring for the self is pursued in order to ensure survival. Morality is seen largely as a matter of sanctions imposed by society from without. Attachment to another with a sense of responsibility eventually triggers a transitional phase in which self as the sole object of concern is recognized as selfish.

(2) "Good" is equated with caring for others. The shift from selfishness to responsibility is a move toward wider social participation, and acceptance of shared norms and expectations of society. The trap here is to see survival as fulfilling others' needs and expectations, an image often held up as the "good woman/wife/sister" etc. Inevitably the desire to please, to resist hurting anyone, leads to conflict and a growing disequilibrium. The tension and confusion of this all-too-familiar mindset roughly corresponds to Kohlberg's stage three of moral development which seeks to hold the need for approval in balance with the desire to care for others. The transition from this perspective in which many women find themselves at mid-life is achieved only when sacrificial devotion to "goodness" in the eyes of others gives way to an inner truth which sees awareness of personal needs as essential and necessary. In a word, one is also responsible to and for oneself.

(3) Goodness moves to truth: Responsible caring includes the self as well as others. This mature stance implies a deeper sense of one's own self-worth, along with an ability to claim the power both to choose and to accept the responsibility for the choices made. Unlike the first level of moral development, obligation to self *includes* obligation to others in relationship, without the destructive or masochistic approach of the second level.

The question is not either/or but both/and. Once this transition is made, the disparity between selfishness and responsibility dissolves. In the inner search for integrity, equality, and honesty, woman ceases to be passively dependent on others for validation.

Our experience of women in mid-life supports Gilligan's research. We see many beginning to move out of Gilligan's second level only in the middle of their lives and the movement is arduous, for they have been so carefully conditioned not to cause pain to another. As Jean Baker Miller writes:

> It is of extreme importance to stress that women have been led to feel that they can integrate and use all their attributes if they use them for others, but *not for themselves*. They have developed the sense that their lives *should* be guided by the constant need to attune themselves to the wishes, desires, and needs of others. The others are the important ones and the guides to action.[4] (Emphasis ours)

Often at mid-life, women begin to recognize that in a messy and ambiguous world we will cause pain, no matter how hard we try to avoid doing so. The woman who has struggled in the first half of her life to be super-mom, nun, or career woman has often unconsciously played the martyr/victim role and been applauded for it. Only when she begins to evaluate who she really is and to determine what *her* values and needs are does she perceive this oppressive situation for what it is. She recognizes the need to make choices, to be responsible, not just for others, but for herself—recognizing that if hurt is inevitable, she can decide where and how that hurt will come, still struggling to be responsible in relationships, but now recognizing that a valid central relationship is the one she has with herself.

This recognition can create havoc in marriages when a wife and/or mother is no longer content to just be care-giver of others. She may choose to work outside the home, finish school or achieve a graduate degree. The husband is often just now learning to appreciate the intimacy of home, whereas the wife is focused on achieving professional or personal success that will make her a more responsible, integrated and honestly loving person. These can be difficult years of mutual adjustment.

In addition, male counselors or spiritual directors are often not prepared for the anger or rage a woman experiences when she gets in touch with the oppressiveness of male-dominated/patriarchal norms in social structures, church, institutions. To many men, the anger seems extreme: "much ado about nothing," or typical female irrationality. On the contrary, it is an important step in women's growth and integration which needs to be respected and dealt with.

Again, understanding Gilligan's critique of all-male studies can help women to understand the tensions, crises, struggles they experience at mid-life. Discovering they do not fit the male norm does not imply something is lacking in them; however, it may seem to. Adult Christian responsibility implies care for oneself, and to disregard this care would ultimately cause more harm for self and others.

We are not implying that women's pattern of moral development is superior but that it is valid. Certainly, in our over-masculinized world it highlights the importance of relationship and the universal need for compassion and care. An ethics abstracted from life (separation) often sacrifices very real persons on the altar of truth. Gilligan's critique points to the need for a more integrated and holistic approach to moral decision-making on the part of all.

Notes

1. Carol Gilligan, *In a Different Voice* (Cambridge, Mass.: Harvard University Press, 1982) p. 12.
2. James W. Fowler, *Becoming Adult, Becoming Christian*, (San Francisco: Harper & Row, 1984) p. 40.
3. Gilligan, *op. cit.*, pp. 74ff.
4. Jean Baker Miller, *Toward a New Psychology of Women* (Boston: Beacon Press, 1976) pp. 60–61.

John Sanford and Fritz Kunkel
on Ego-Centricity

The writings of John Sanford, episcopal priest-Jungian analyst, rely heavily both on his Jungian background and his deep Christian roots. In *Ministry Burnout*,[1] in a section dependent on Fritz Kunkel, Sanford develops a model for understanding the characteristic Jungian belief that the emergence of the Self is always a painful loss for the ego. The brief synthesis of his material offers another way of looking at the challenges and creative possibilities of mid-life. Sanford's psychological model also involves a faith-stance, for it develops a concrete way of understanding Jesus' invitation: "If anyone wants to be a follower of mine, let that one renounce self and take up the cross and follow me" (Mk 8:34).

With Jung, Sanford believes that the basis of a religious psychology or spirituality is found in the individuation process, the development of a personality that is undivided, in which the warring parts are reconciled and the conscious and unconscious are in harmony. Put more simply, spirituality consists in becoming what God intended us to become. In keeping with the realization that we are not totally in control of the process, that the roots of the transition are not truly conscious—the transformation happens to us. The process is more Divine work than human. As we grow we do become more conscious of self (who I am, never finished, but on-the-way), of relationships (all our interactions with others), and of God (or the overall meaning of our life). But we cannot do this ourselves; it is the work of grace; we can cooperate or resist.

Maturity and the work of grace have a single aim—the developing of our human capacity to love others, a gradual, persistent shifting of our reference from *I* to *We*. Put in Jungian terms, with Sanford and his guide, Kunkel, this means overcoming *ego-centricity*, literally growing out of concentration on one's own ego-centric stance toward life to enter more deeply into knowledge of self and relationship with others and with God. Concerned with its own defense and the fulfillment of ego drives and ambitions, the ego inevitably protects itself.

In a rather playful schema, Kunkel, and later Sanford, suggest four "Ego-Centric patterns," ways the ego has learned to survive, ways that need to be put aside if self is to be realized, if individuation is to happen, if we are to learn to love. We have learned ways to get along in the world. As we get older and approach the apparent chaos of mid-life, our survival techniques begin to fail us. They are no longer adequate. We can try to protect them, or we can let go and let a full self, a full person emerge.

Much of the discomfort of mid-life involves the process of this death as the self emerges. Our patterns of behavior no longer work. We need to die to one (inadequate) self-identity to discover another fuller one.

The four ego-centric patterns that Sanford offers us are stereotypes; they will never come in pure form. They are suggestive ways of coping with life. Each of us will tend to rely on one more than others. Each of us will have, in a sense, inherited one pattern from the type of family environment in which we were raised and our response to that environment.

The Clinging Vine. Raised in a soft, indulgent environment, and overly sensitive to this environment, the *pam-*

pered child grows into an adult posture of dependence, an inability to stand on her[2] own. She will be inclined to lean on another or on an institution. She will go through life with a strong need for something or someone to stand by. The clinging vine will be either very good or very needy, and preferably both, in creating volunteers to take care of her. "Minus 100," or the failing chaos of this ego-centric state, occurs when there is no longer anyone to support her, and she is forced by others, who have perhaps grown tired of the game, to stand on her own feet.

The Star: Also raised in a soft, indulgent, overly permissive environment, with vitality, aggressiveness, and some talent, the *admired* child grows into an adult who needs center stage, admiration, acclaim. The star is secure in this ego-centric pattern as long as the applause continues. If no one pays attention or a second star arrives on the scene, her crisis begins. She can always star at being good. No matter how successful she may be, the star always tends to know, somewhere in her untapped unconscious that she is a bit of a fake. "Minus 100," or the chaotic demise of this ego-centric state, begins with real failure, total, or an apparently total, inadequacy.

The Turtle: Raised in a harsh, brutal environment, and lacking in vitality, the *rejected* (or *injured*) child becomes an adult with a soft underbelly, a hard outer shell. He is a person threatened by life, whose real emotional life is hidden. He is never really (visibly) hurt or vulnerable and is inclined to extreme emotional or physical withdrawal. He is not going anywhere, and nothing ever really gets lived. The turtle is a genuine victim of life who has been severely wounded, perhaps many times, along the way. Life is filled with situations that must be overcome. "Minus 100," or the chaotic breakdown of this ego-centric pattern, occurs when the turtle is no longer able to hide and must now show his emotional life—there is no longer anywhere to run.

The Nero (Tyrant): Also raised in a harsh, brutal environment, but with vitality and aggressiveness, the *self-assertive, brutalized* child becomes the dominating adult, who moves through life surviving by controlling others. Unlike the star, Nero does not need to be center stage as long as he has power; he may be found behind the scenes manipulating everyone. He must be in control and tends to live in a paranoid state regarding others as a threat to his power. "Minus 100," chaos, occurs when people no longer accept being mastered and Nero is challenged to enter into relationships with them.

For all of us, our capacity to love is in proportion to our resolution of these basic ego-centric states. Only by surrendering the false security they offer can we enter relationally into adult life. The mid-life transition can then be described as the struggle to surrender the ego-centric state with which we have learned to cope so far, in order to enter into the next part of life fully human, fully relational.

Clearly, we can shift back and forth, be different at work than at home (e.g., Nero in the office becomes a turtle at home). The types tend to bond together for survival (e.g., Star marries a Clinging Vine). Much of mid-life marriage struggle results from the effort of one type to change in ways with which the other cannot cope (e.g., the Turtle will no longer cringe before the Nero; the Clinging Vine no longer gives the Star the ego-strokes she requires).

Obviously, this schema oversimplifies the complexity of the human personality, human growth, human struggle. However, it does provide a framework for understanding the pain, tension, dis-ease of mid-life when the way in which we have learned to survive and apparently to thrive no longer works, no longer enables us to deal with others and the world. The schema helps us understand what it means to die in order to live, to renounce something dear in oneself, and it makes a concrete reality out of the cross that is unique to each of us (Mk 8:34).

A final, helpful insight growing out of these patterns of ego-centric stances concerns what Jung calls the shadow which we treated earlier. In this schema, this repressed, unrecognized shadow contains 90% pure gold, for the things the Clinging Vine or Nero represses are the things that do not fit the ego-centric pattern they have developed. These repressed dimensions of the personality, if embraced, would help make the person whole. Hence, embracing the shadow, letting in what has previously been shut out of consciousness, becomes essential to human growth and the blossoming of one's capacity to love.

Each of us can find ourselves in these ego-centric patterns and perhaps better understand the mid-life struggle we experience.

Notes

1. John Sanford, *Ministry Burnout* (Paulist Press, New York, 1982) pp. 6–71. This section of the book elaborates Fritz Kunkel's theory of ego-centric states. Our material relies on Sanford/Kunkel from *Ministry Burnout,* as well as an unpublished lecture given by John Sanford in Tacoma, Washington, July 1983. No effort is made to exactly identify each page of this source on which we rely.

2. Each ego-centric pattern is found in both men and women. For simplicity, we present two in feminine language, two in male, using the same division Sanford himself does.

6

Daniel Levinson, Adapted for Men and Women

In 1978, Daniel Levinson published *The Seasons of A Man's Life*[1] which has become the paradigmatic book on mid-life, at least for men. Levinson's original reserch, an enormous sociological sample, included women as well as men, though his final work focused only on the transition of three different social classes of males (executives, laborers, artists). In presenting this material, we recognize that the categories are primarily drawn from male experience and the conclusions are likely to be most apt for men. However, after offering this material in several classes and suggesting this schema to women as well, we suggest that much of the material, as we have reshaped it, has to do with the human project at mid-life and is common to both sexes. We invite women to consider whether this material is appropriate to their journey and to see it as helpful in understanding their spouses and their friends.

Although Levinson's entire book is relevant to our discussions and helps to provide other models for understanding the experiences at mid-life, we will focus only on that section which deals specifically with the mid-life project.[2] Levinson suggests three major tasks at mid-life:

1. To review and reappraise one's life so far.
2. Not so much to begin the next stage as to modify negative elements of the past and test new choices.
3. To deal with the polarities that can be sources of deep division in the self.

Although review and reappraisal and the modification of behavior are significant and will be treated often elsewhere in this book, we will concentrate on Levinson's third task, the struggle to reconcile the polarities of human life that become critical at this time. To us, this reconciliation of polarities provides a model of understanding the mid-life transition that seems most helpful in Levinson's work and most applicable to women and men alike. We rely more on his outline, adapting it as we see it played out in all our lives. So we invite you, male or female, to consider the reality of these polarities in life.

POLARITIES IN HUMAN LIFE, ESPECIALLY SIGNIFICANT AT MID-LIFE

A. Young/old:

In the middle of our lives, we all recognize that we are no longer young. Our bodies begin to fail us, our energy wanes, our concentration and memory diminish. Yet we are not old. We are still vital, alive, perhaps much more competent in some areas than we ever have been. The challenge of mid-life is not to collapse this tension. We need not become prematurely old, dying a long time before our death, nor need we desperately hold onto youth, obstinately denying the aging process. We struggle to hold on to the values of both youth and age: to be young speaks of new birth, growth, possibility, initiation; to be old speaks of termination, fruition, stability, convenient patterns, completion, and perhaps some form of death and new life. Each has values. Each is part of the middle of life. The ability to reconcile the best of both, without giving in to either, is a central opportunity of our middle years.

All of us have seen the middle-aged person desperately

hold onto youth—the shirt unbuttoned to the navel, the newly acquired beads, the youthful faddish clothes, the dyed hair, the total involvement in one's children's successes at little league or ballet.

We have also seen ourselves or our friends age prematurely before our eyes, no longer interested in "going out," afraid to try new things, unable to adjust to children leaving home, or watching younger men and women being promoted past them in the market place. The tension is real and pervasive. We think sadly of a mother who had been alive, vital, vibrant, caring not just for her children but all their friends as well, who rapidly and literally died when her children left home. She had never cared for herself by developing new interests or accomplishments.

In the middle of our lives, we do indeed face reality in a variety of new forms. We do change; our bodies, energy, strength, sleep, memory are all different. Our parents die and leave us as the generation "in charge." Our friends begin to die. We are faced with our own mortality, and our desire for immortality, though possibly unconscious, becomes so very real. In the face of this new sense of mortality, great religious possibilities arise.

In this tension between young and old wrestling in the lives of each of us, possibilities abound. What have we learned, what have we become that we can pass on? What is a *legacy* that we can share with those who follow us? Is there a book we need to write, a wisdom we want to share?

Parenthetically, the two of us began to write books and articles as each of us moved into middle-age; only later as we began to familiarize ourselves with this mid-life material did we realize the desire to leave a legacy that prompted our new mid-life creativity.

Besides the desire to leave some legacy, at mid-life we will often be inclined to become, in the best sense, *mentors* of those half-a-generation younger than ourselves. We find ourselves, almost unnoticed, slipping into one or several relationships with others who seem interested in sharing our experience and our wisdom.

Perhaps as mentors, perhaps by means of a legacy, each of us needs to come to grips with this young/old polarity in the middle of our lives.

B. Destruction/creation:

The basic question of the destruction/creation polarity asks: How do I deal creatively with hurts I have caused and that others have caused me? In the middle of our lives each of us has, in Pogo's words, "met the enemy and it is us!" We recognize that we have not lived up to our possibilities, our dreams. We have caused real harm to others, our children, our students, our clients, our parents, our friends. We have let people down, and, mostly, we have disappointed ourselves. We have not written the great American novel, achieved financial stability, produced the most successful or adjusted children, or become as holy or as loving as we had hoped.

No one arrives at mid-life without some scars, without the realization of some significant failure. Each of us is tempted to give up, surrender, admit defeat before the overwhelming and apparently victorious challenge of life. Many are tempted, on the other hand, to deny inadequacies and continue to wear the mask of "perfection" before others. We can refuse to admit our weakness or be defeated by it. This polarity invites us to do neither, but rather to manage the disappointment and to affirm the good, honest fruitfulness and grace of our life so far, reconciling and forgiving ourselves and others.

Our task is neither to retire, nor to ignore, but to affirm both the good and the bad—to go on with life creatively despite a broken marriage that we expected to last forever, or an imperfect marriage, or life-choice that will never satisfy our deepest longings. We struggle to continue loving our children even though they have not made us as proud as we would like. We try to do our best and most conscientious work even though others are better, more productive, faster than ourselves. And we do this because we come to know where we truly have been successes: the children who have recognized our imperfect but real love, the person wounded by life who has carried on because of our support, the cause that we have successfully championed for years.

In terms of Christian faith, we have now for the first time the possibility of real faith which knows that, yes, we are indeed sinners, but we are loved, called, chosen, redeemed sinners and there are no other kind of folks—only wounded people like ourselves who are loved by God. We can recognize that we have in some form, at some times, even with a degree of heroism, responded to this love and call. At midlife we can authentically begin becoming saints, able truly to know both our need for and the presence of a Redeemer in our lives. Holding together the tension of creative and destructive capabilities in ourselves, we can, perhaps for the first time, live in response to having been loved first by God, no longer in a desperate misguided effort to somehow win God's favor by our perfection.

C. Masculine/feminine:[3]

In the language of Jung, all human persons are androgynous, containing within themselves the fullness of both femininity and masculinity, having the capacity for the best traits of each gender. The sexually developed person will be both strong and tender, gentle and assertive, able to feel and to think. Jung, as we have seen, uses the terms *animus* and *anima* to speak about this reality, this polarity. He asserts that every man has within his unconscious an *anima,* or undeveloped host of feminine possibilities that can be released and incorporated into his adult, mid-life personality. Every woman has within her unconscious an *animus,* or undeveloped host of male characteristics, possibilities that can be integrated into her fully adult personality.

Discussing this material, Jung seems to fall heir to dangerous cultural, environmental stereotypes, describing the *anima* in terms often derogatory to women, and the *animus* in terms overly complimentary to men. Jung seems to be no more able than anyone else to accurately describe what are "feminine traits" or "masculine characteristics." Still, somewhere in our consciousness we know that some reality persists. Each of us does need to incorporate into adult life the characteristics of both sexes, which were left undeveloped in earlier years.

The stereotypes are operative sometimes and must be admitted and worked with. The man whose younger life has been almost entirely involved in an outer world, making a name for himself, being aggressive and assertive, needs to learn to stay around the house and grow flowers or bake cookies if he is to become whole. The woman who has stayed home, raised children, kept a house, may desperately need to "move out," get a job, establish her autonomy and professional capabilities in the middle of her life. Men and women do often cross paths at this time of life, losing each other in the process. Just when the wife is ready to go out and deal with a larger, outer world, the husband is ready to spend more time at home, developing his interior and reflective sides. The polarity can and does present itself in ways that men and women have traditionally and typically developed.

However, as our world changes, our roles become less

paralyzing. Particular human gifts are developed not along expected sexual lines, but on fully human ones. As women become vice-presidents and priests, as men become house-husbands or florists, the task of integrating all our human, sexually-based traits endures. The form changes; the project remains.

For example, a man who has always been part of an all-male religious community in his adult life has always had people around to run things, make decisions, be assertive. He has in earlier years been able to develop his poetic, sensitive side. Such development helps, in fact, to work out a balance among the members of the male community in which he lives. In the middle of his life he has a dream: he sees himself at a basketball game, ready to play, extremely "hot," putting in shots from every corner with amazing aplomb. He is aware that he is no longer young. He may not be able to play the entire game, no matter how great a player he is. As tip-off time approaches, he realizes that each team is made up of both men and women. The other team has four men and two women. His team has four women and two men. He is aware that the rules of this particular game insist that each team play with two men and one woman—which means that he, at forty-five, will have to play the entire game. Waking, he understands that he is unequipped here in the middle of his life. He cannot take part with energy and expertise because he has not adequately developed his "masculine" side. Growth, integration, balance for him, the reconciliation of *animus* and *anima* polarities, consists not in developing the stereotypical "feminine" traits, but in learning to be assertive, aggressive, decisive. The experience of this individual man is repeated in countless variations all inviting balance out of the varied experiences of our early life.

The point is clear. Fully rounded, human, sexual development constitutes a central task of mid-life whatever the unique terms of that development may be.

Men may find themselves in the middle of their lives confronted by an inner or an outer woman telling them "That's not it at all," telling them that their development, the person they have become is inadequate. They may return from their quest for the Holy Grail, their struggle with the outside world, thinking they had succeeded, only to be told that they have done it all wrong, looked in the wrong places, struggled with the wrong realities. They need now, in the middle of their lives, again to begin learning that friendship, intimacy, relationships are more important than tasks.

Women may find that their lifelong effort to make peace with everyone, to keep things harmonious and personal, to create no enemies and cause no suffering was a mistaken venture. They may discover in middle years that one cannot move through life without hurting anyone, and the real challenge is to take charge of their life, to know their own needs and gifts, to become responsible for the choices they make which may necessarily involve some hurt to others.

Superficially, and stereotypically at mid-life, a man shifts from achieving to relating; a woman shifts from nurturing to penetrating, constructing. In reality, each needs to learn to do both, and the tensions of male-female are unique to each individual depending on how his or her earlier life developed.

D. Attachment/separation:

Many of the personal letters we quoted in a previous chapter spoke of a struggle between the need for intimacy and the need to be alone, the tension between time for oneself in apparent opposition to time for the needs of others and community. In the middle of our lives this polarity, this tension must also be resolved. We probably emphasized one part of the polarity as we grew into adulthood. Most people exaggerate their involvement with and dependence on others. In whatever way we develop, each of us needs at this stage of life to balance off, to work out some compromise, in order to both "be with," and "be alone."

In most cases, especially with men, this involves a growing ability to lead an inner life, to be reflective, prayerful. This development is by no means easy. Men often find it difficult to be still, especially if nothing happens. We fear that many men stop any growth at this time, unable to stand the quiet and the emptiness after a busy and apparently productive life. Women, by and large, have provided for such spaces in their lives, even if only in snatches.

Young religious are often baffled by the tendency of older priests or sisters to take their afternoon recreation time alone. The younger people cannot imagine going on long solitary afternoon strolls when there are people to be with or games to be played. As youths turn older, the chance for such walks in solitude seem rare and priceless.

Each of us needs to develop our imagination, our fantasy, our ability to play, even alone. These capacities are the fruit of necessary quiet time. So, a central task of mid-life consists in developing the balance between needs of self and the needs of society.

If one has kept to oneself a great deal in early years, the mid-life project becomes to enter more fully, forcefully and responsibly into life. The recluse will not become a social reformer, in most cases. But the shy, reticent individual can discover ways to assume some identification with and responsibility for a larger than private world. We know of one shy young man moving into his forties who has joined Amnesty International and spends a large part of his previously secluded time writing letters on behalf of political prisoners. Again, whatever our previous development has been, a balance needs to be achieved at this time.

CONCLUSION: A REFLECTION ON CHANGE

Levinson's polarities offer us another way, another model to reflect on chaos as well as the creation that occurs at mid-life. Certainly, these polarities do not offer a solution, any more than any other model. While they may help to explain, they do not explain away the tension, fear, discomfort we feel. Each of them requires some change in us if balance is to be achieved. Change is always awkward, always difficult. The shy student in high school, trying to be more aggressive, forward, does so clumsily at first. Her lack of perfect grace calls attention to itself. She is tempted to retreat, withdraw back to the accustomed behavior, to be again the way everyone perceives her to be. This same awkwardness is even more discomforting in mid-life. We will be noticed as we struggle to change. People had become used to us as we were. We will call attention to ourselves. Others, perhaps those closest to us, will subtly or directly invite us to go back and be as we have been, as they have known us. We will be tempted to comply. In his wonderful book, *Transitions*,[4] Robert Bridges suggests some very practical ways to live through the awkward time of change, the period of "already now," but "not quite yet." He speaks about the "neutral zone," that period between. When we lose something, it is natural to try to replace it as quickly as possible. We want to recover our youthful vitality, so we exhaust ourselves working out. We are so anxious to get another job to replace the one that did not suit us anymore—or another wife, or husband. But, Bridges asserts, we need to trust the waiting time between jobs, relationships, burning interests. Our friends may often try to hasten us, get us to date, or work, or come out of our necessary shell. We may be unsure ourselves whether we are going crazy or becoming enlightened, but we need to allow ourselves the time.

During this period in between as we let go of one way of being and move towards discovering another, Bridges suggests several helpful steps:

- We can find a regular time and place to be alone.
- We can write an autobiography, telling, for ourselves, the meaning of our life so far.
- We can ask ourselves: What would be unfinished for me if my life ended now? What do I really want to be or accomplish before I die? (Such questions can help us focus on the direction we want or need to choose.)
- We can make an extended retreat, going off somewhere alone, refusing to stay busy and avoid or delay the completion of our transition.

We would add to Bridges' excellent suggestions the further advice to be sure to have someone to talk to, perhaps a professional, a pastoral counselor, a spiritual director, but certainly someone, a trusted friend, a confidant. As in every part of life, we cannot make this journey toward balance alone.

In the previous sections we have offered a variety of models along psychological, existential, experiential lines to help look at the challenge, the invitation, the tasks of midlife. Again, we invite you to pause and reflect on each and see if our suggested tasks or those given us by "authorities" are your tasks. How do they fit into your life? Do these struggles match or clarify your honest wrestlings?

In the following pages we will continue to break open the reality of the mid-life passage, trying to discover what it is that we all experience. Now we will begin to look at the experience more specifically as a religious journey of, and in, faith—we see the crisis as a religious crisis, literally, a time of judgment, an opportunity for growth toward deeper life in God.

Notes

1. Daniel J. Levinson, *The Seasons of a Man's Life* (Ballantine Books, New York, 1978). No effort will be made to identify each item of Levinson's material. We do rely heavily on his outline but have made much of it our own.

2. *Ibid.*, pp. 191–260.

3. Here especially we retain Levinson's category but depart from his treatment. This material is our own effort to make sense today out of the *animus/anima* polarity.

4. William Bridges, *Transitions* (Addison-Wesley, Reading, Mass., 1980) pp. 112-31.

PART II

The Mid-Life Experience in Terms of Faith:
A Religious Experience

From Scripture and Poetic Tradition

Thou art indeed just, Lord, if I contend
With thee; but, sir, so what I plead is just.
Why do sinner's ways prosper? and why must
Disappointment all I endeavor end?
　Wert thou my enemy, O thou my friend,
How wouldst thou worse, I wonder, than thou dost
Defeat, thwart me? Oh, the sots and thralls of lust
Do in spare hours more thrive than I that spend,
Sir, life upon thy cause. See, banks and brakes
Now, leaved how thick! Laced they are again
With fretty chervil, look, and fresh wind shakes
Them; birds build—but not I build; no, but strain,
Time's eunuch, and not breed one work that wakes.
Mine, O thou Lord of Life, send my roots rain.[1]

In this chapter we offer a variety of religious reflections on mid-life, hoping, again, not to solve the problems but to surround them, describe them, give some words to help us comprehend our shared, if always unique experience. What is it that is happening to us? We may not express our reality as these authors do, but as we come to understand their words, we can understand ourselves.

　The poet Hopkins, for example, in the middle of his life, voices the often-shared desire to understand why our lives, however religious, prayerful, faith-filled, feel so empty and meaningless now. Why is it that others, who lead less authentic lives, seem to prosper, and everything we do turns to dust and ashes in our mouth? Why does it seem that God has abandoned us, left us to our own weakness, when others in their spare time seem to prosper so much more? Why are we so barren when spring comes to life all around us? Why, when everything else is giving birth, are we so sterile? And which of us at mid-life, with this poet, has not pleaded in silent longing for God's rain to come to our dried-up roots?

Hopkins offers one way of looking at our experience. Here are others from our biblical roots.

THE BOOK OF LAMENTATIONS

The third chapter of the Book of Lamentations offers a classic articulation of mid-life transition. The author writes at the nadir of Jewish history. The Israelites had been conquered by the Babylonians and suffered the loss of temple, land, and glory as a people. This national scene mirrors the inner life of the author who feels keenly the absence of God in his own personal suffering and tragedy.

There are three movements in this painful journaling. The first is the reality of pain and suffering, the experience of nothingness. From the opening line, "I am the man that hath seen (experienced) affliction by the rod of his wrath,"[2] until the sixteenth verse, there is a repeated hammering out of his suffering at Yahweh's hands:

"He has driven and brought me into darkness without any light."

"He has . . . broken my bones."

"He has walled me about."

"He shuts out my prayer."

"He has blocked my ways with hewn stones."

Similes convey his disillusionment with God: "like a bear lying in wait," or "like a lion in hiding." In such experience of confusion and anguish, the religious person at mid-life perceives God as "punisher," the one who causes the suffering. Life experiences call one's inadequate images of God into question.

Verses seventeen and eighteen describe a stage of existential despair, the individual's breaking point:

> My soul bereft of peace,
> I have forgotten what happiness is:
> So I say, "Gone is my glory,
> and my expectation from the Lord."

The following verse is not unlike Jesus' cry on the cross as the poet directs an anguished plea to God: "Remember my affliction and my bitterness, the wormwood and the gall!"

The lines that follow are key to the freeing possibility of mid-life:

> Remember my affliction and my bitterness,
> the wormwood and the gall!
> My soul continually thinks of it
> and is bowed down within me;
> But this I call to mind,
> and therefore I have hope.

The poet recalls the affliction and bitterness that force his soul to bow down within him. The realization of his vulnerability, anguish, and inability to cope forces him to rely totally on God. His own kind of death by existential despair becomes the very ground from which springs tentative life and he says ". . . therefore I have hope."

Despair moves into faith, and disillusionment into hope. His personal myth breaks, the image of himself as in control, able to deal with all life's vicissitudes. One who experiences this mid-life void—the way of negativity and non-being—comes to accept this situation of no meaning, no reality, and still trusts that eventually life will emerge. Once the experience is accepted, the journey inward to freedom and integration can continue. The poet's realization that God is greater than his own strength (which he experiences as impotence) leads him to rely on God's compassion and faithfulness: ". . . therefore I have hope."

Verses twenty-five to thirty offer a reflective meditation on this suffering and *his* interpretation of it. He recalls from past experience that the Lord is good to those who seek him and who quietly wait for salvation. The agitation and fright of the first eighteen verses have given way to the statement that "It is good for man that he bear the yoke," that he ". . . sit alone and keep silence." If this is done there ". . . may be hope." For the suffering has become creative and the poet seeks to learn its lesson and to profit from it. He neither merely resigns himself to enduring, nor seeks to anesthetize it. Loneliness, depression, anxiety can be opportunities for growth if accepted and embraced as a means to greater wholeness and integration.

The dynamic of the religious person at mid-life can be the same as that of the poet of Lamentations, who moves from an experience of nothingness to a despair that breaks the myth of the conscious self (who I see myself to be), into a realization of greater freedom and a sense of a compassionate God-with-us on the entire journey.

JOB

> Did you notice my servant Job? There is no one like
> him on the earth; a sound and honest man who fears
> God and shuns evil (Jb 1:8).

The story of Job, primarily concerned with the question of evil, struggles without resolution with the world's most ancient question: Why does the good person suffer? But as we consider God's servant Job, we will do well to recall that Job was in the middle of his life when the story begins. He had spent the first half of his life building up an empire, a good self-image, a home, family, health, wealth, love, respectability, and a deep, deep faith. And God rewarded Job for his goodness. As a person in command, in control, responsive to God's will (which coincided so closely with his own), Job, like every human person, experiences a very different reality as he moves into his middle years.

That Job had been a good and successful person there is no doubt. With some justification he tells us of his greatness:

> When I went out to the gate of the city,
> > when I took my seat in the square,
> As soon as I appeared, the young men stepped aside,
> > while the older men rose to their feet.
> Men of note interrupted their speeches . . . .
> The voices of rulers were silent. . . .
> They waited anxiously to hear me . . .
> They waited for me, as men wait for rain,
> > open-mouthed, as if to catch the year's last showers.
> If I smiled at them, it was too good to be true,
> > they watched my face for the least sign of favor.
> In a lordly style, I told them which course to take,
> > and like a king amid his armies
> > I led them where I chose.
> My praises echoed in every ear,
> > and never an eye but smiled on me:
> Because I freed the poor man when he called,
> > and the orphan who had no one to help him.
> When men were dying, I it was who had their blessing;
> > if widows' hearts rejoiced, that was my doing.
> I had dressed myself in righteousness like a garment. . . .
> I was eyes for the blind and feet for the lame. . . .

So I thought to myself, 'I shall die in honor . . .' (Jb 29:7–
18.

Job, the perfect Jewish man, cared for the widows, the
orphans, the strangers in his midst! He had done everything
in his control to please his God and himself.
But all is stripped away; he loses everything. One after
another, wealth, health, family disappear. Job is tempted to
curse God and die. His comforters become his tempters
(perhaps, really, the inner voices in Job himself, or in us)
encouraging him to look carefully and discover and admit
his sin. What had he done wrong to deserve such a dire fate?
Job is forced to review his entire life story, to tell it over from
another vantage point. Much of the long poem involves this
temptation, this retelling, as Job searches for the blame that
must be his. Finally, in all honesty, Job can find no cause
for such misery. Still, he does not really know; he cannot
tell. He is uncertain of anything any longer.
Job is reduced by pain and loss to the near despair of
many at mid-life:

. . . months of delusion I have assigned to me,
nothing for my own but nights of grief.
Lying in bed I wonder, "When will it be day?"
Risen I think, "How slowly evening comes" (7:3–4).

And later:

If I say, "My bed will comfort me,
    my couch will soothe my pain,"
You frighten me with dreams,
    and terrify me with visions (7:13–14).

He complains to God:

> Suppose I have sinned, what have I done to you,
> you tireless watcher of mankind? (7:20).

Poor Job, his plans fallen apart, his dreams shattered, must question, with us all, who really is in control: "My days have passed far otherwise than I had planned" (17:21). He can discover no real cause, no answer, no solution to the misery he now knows. Finally, he no longer seeks to know, or understand. He asks of his friends, his comforters, not answers, but compassion: "Pity me, pity me, you, my friends" (19:21).

Job holds on tenaciously to some remnant of faith, some vestige of the confidence in a God he so casually trusted in his earlier years:

> This I know: that my Avenger lives,
> and he, the last will take his stand on earth.
> After my awaking, he will set me close to him,
> and from my flesh I shall look on God.
> He whom I shall see will take my part,
> these eyes will gaze on him, and find him, not aloof
> (19:25–27).

Finally, Job is led to surrender to a God he cannot understand, control, manipulate:

> My words have been frivolous: what can I reply?
> I had better lay my finger on my lips.
> I have spoken once . . . I will not speak again:
> more than once, I will add nothing (40:4–5).

> I know that you are all powerful:
> what you conceive, you can perform.
> I am the man who obscured your designs,
> with my empty headed words.

I have been holding forth on matters I cannot understand,
on marvels beyond my knowledge. . . .
I knew you then only by hearsay:
but now, having seen you with my own eyes,
I retract all I have said,
and in dust and ashes I repent (42:2–6).

In order for us, contemporary people, to draw fruit from this marvelous story, our faith perspective need not ascribe to a God who *does* all these things to Job, nor to a God who would enter into such a wager with the devil, leaving poor Job a helpless pawn. The story makes complete sense without being a story of Job the tennis ball batted back and forth by two external powers. The story of Job is simply the story of everyone written in italics; his experience is shared, in miniature, by all of us.

Perhaps it helps to recognize this if we realize that the ending for the story of the Book of Job was a later addition to the original. In the biblical narrative now, after his repentance, Job gets everything back—wife, family, riches beyond what he had in the beginning. He is more blessed than before. If the story ends only with Job's surrender to God, the real nature of the richest blessing may be better understood, for the best reward Job gets may better be seen as a new attitude toward life, toward himself, toward others, and toward God.

The Book of Job offers a universal story of the mid-life crisis, larger perhaps than our own, but significantly similar. If such can happen to Job, then why not to us? If Job can be so destroyed and distraught, cannot we? If he can endure the doubt and darkness, cannot we? If he can survive this midnight and wait to discover dawn, cannot we? If he can discover a deeper and more personal relationship with his God ("Now, having seen you with my eyes") that goes far beyond the hearsay of his youth, is it not worth in plenteous measure such sustaining hope in us? And, parenthetically perhaps, as we watch our friends or loved ones endure a singularly dark time in their lives and we are called as "comforters," can we be present in silent compassion—a waiting, hoping presence, with no answers but love? The Book of Job invites us to consider these and similar questions, providing us with an excellent model of the mid-life passage, for Job is one of us.

PETER

While we are looking at scriptural models of mid-life, consider for a moment the passage with which we began this book. In the final chapter of John's Gospel, the risen Christ takes Peter aside from the others—Peter whom he still called to be shepherd of his flock. In his earlier days Peter had been brash, bold, confident, trusting in his own resources—a sword he did not need, a courage he did not have. Now he has experienced resurrection, death and rebirth with Jesus. Chastened, he cannot say he loves Jesus "*more* than these others do," but only "You know I love you" (Jn 21:15). It is in this context that Jesus says:

> . . . when you were young
> you put on your own belt
> and walked where you liked.
> But when you grow old
> you will stretch out your hands,
> and somebody else will put a belt around you
> and take you where you would rather not go (21:18).

From now on Peter, transformed by sharing in the death and resurrection of Jesus, will be more led than in charge. Perhaps to see the greatest miracle Jesus worked, far beyond healing of paralysis or blindness, even beyond lifting up of one physically dead, we need only consider Peter. Compare the Peter of the Acts of the Apostles with the Peter of the Gospel stories. In Acts, "giving what he has in the name of Jesus" (3:6), Peter is confident not in himself, but in the Spirit of God, and he has a power not his own but from the Lord. Peter, too, looked at from this vantage point, becomes a story of hope in the middle of our lives.

Three wonderful poems offer other reflections on the religious dimension of mid-life experience. The first, another poem by Gerard Manley Hopkins, will be followed by poems from John Shea and Thomas Merton.

HOPKINS

Not, I'll not, carrion comfort, despair, not feast on thee;
Not untwist—slack they may be—these last strands of man
In me or, most weary cry I can no more. I can:
Can something, hope, wish day come, not choose not to be.
But ah, but O thou terrible, why wouldst thou rude on me
They wring-world right foot rock? lay a lionlimb against
    me? scan
With darksome devouring eyes my bruised bones? and fan,
O in turns of temptest, me heaped there; me frantic to
    avoid thee and flee?
Why? That my chaff might fly; my grain lie, sheer and
    clear.
Nay in all that toil, that coil, since (seems) I kissed the rod,
Hand rather, my heart lo! lapped strength, stole joy, would
    laugh, cheer.
Cheer whom though? the hero whose heaven-handling
    flung me, foot trod
Me? or me that fought him? O which one? is it each one?
    That night, that year

Of now done darkness I, wretch, lay wrestling with (my
God!) my God.[3]

In the darkest moment, one can choose not to despair,
can refuse to give up, can "not choose not to be," rejecting
the suicidal option. Hopkins, a convert, cannot understand
why since he entered into life with God ("kissed the rod,
hand rather") his life has been riddled with turmoil, tossed
about by the (apparent) action of that very Redeemer. But,
underneath the turmoil, the temptation, the inclination to
give in to the flesh-eating comfort of despair, lies the vague
but deep recognition that, like Jacob, it is his God he wrestles with. Where Hopkins once could choose the direction
of his life, now control is being wrested from him, and now
not just his church, his faith, his Jesuit vocation, but his entire life is in the hands of another, his God.

JOHN SHEA

Prayer for the Long Haul

> Allow me not, Lord of Blood
> to be one with the one
> and mountaintop smile
> on the trashing plain.
> Allow me not, Lord of Bone,
> to drive out ambition with a whip of dreams
> and smuggle heaven onto the troubled earth.
> Allow me not, Lord of Flesh,
> escape ecstasy, the inner endless journey,
> the noiseless perfections of the soul.
> Give me, Broken Lord, the long courage
> for compromised truths, small justices,
> partial peaces.
> Keep my soul in my teeth, hold me in hope,

and teach me to fight
the way farmers with hoes defeat armies
and rolled up manuscripts survive wars.[4]

Shea prays in the middle of his life for realism, a prayer
of one who has dreamed extravagantly and experienced the
less than perfect; he has come to know the truth that "the
greatest enemy of the good is the perfect," and "if something is worth doing at all, it's worth doing poorly." He prays
not to let his faith become an isolating thing that separates
him from blood, flesh, and brokenness, where the Lord is
truly found. He prays to be able to live with the destruction
and creation in his life, and to accept and rejoice in *truth,*
however compromised, *justice,* however small, *peace,* however partial. He prays in the ambiguous reality of middle life
as we must all learn to pray, "for the long haul."

THOMAS MERTON

A touching mid-life poem from Thomas Merton speaks
also to this destruction/creation tension with some of the
darkness that Hopkins knew and the struggle to maintain
composure before an "absent" God.

This afternoon, let me be a
sad person. Am I not
permitted (like other men)
to be sick of myself?

Am I not allowed to be hollow
or fall into the hole
or break my bones (within me)
in the trap set by my own
lie to myself? O my friend,
I too must sin and sin.

I too must hurt other people and
(since I am no exception)
I must be hated by them.

Do not forbid me, therefore,
to taste the same bitter poison,
and drink the gall that love
(love most of all) so easily becomes.

Do not forbid me (once again) to be
angry, bitter, disillusioned,
wishing I could die.

While life and death are
killing one another in my flesh,
leave me in peace. I can enjoy,
even as other men, this agony.

Only (whoever you may be)
pray for my soul. Speak my name
to Him, for in my bitterness
I can hardly speak to Him, and He
While He is busy killing me
refuses to listen.[5]

Perhaps a word or two of this is yours as well. As we
move from the controlled, neat tidy lives we may have led
into a much more messy room, we long to be allowed our
messiness, whoever we may be. Others may insist that we
"shape up," be as we once were, are expected to be. But for
a transition time we may need to grovel in our weakness,
experience without pretense the absence of our God, and
show to all the world the anger, bitterness, and disillusionment we had so carefully hidden from others and ourselves.

CONCLUSION

After these glimpses of mid-life from Scripture and literature, we turn to a somewhat more structured religious reflection on the mid-life reality, searching still for hints about the spiritual dimensions of this journey. In an excellent article on "Nothingness and Psycho-spiritual Growth," William Kraft suggests:

> The apparent loss of meaning (often experienced in mid-life) is actually a quest for integral relatedness, creative growth, and permanent fulfillment. The yearning of loneliness is a springboard to the togetherness of love.
> The solitude of aloneness is the place of self-discovery in service of self-surrender.
> The emptiness of depression is a search for the fulfillment of joy.
> The change that stirs anxiety is a movement towards a permanence of commitment.
> The groundlessness of dread is a preparation for solidity of courage.
> The dark burden of guilt is a summons to the lightsomeness of autonomy.
> The lethargy of boredom is a thirst for the vitality of enthusiasm.
> The lifelessness of apathy is a retreat for the sake of re-entry into life.
> The pain of anguish is a breakdown for the breakthrough of God.[6]

Kraft invites us to view what can be seen as problems as a host of opportunities, and to view crisis as a chance for change, chaos as the birthplace of creation.

Mid-life offers opportunities for fuller, deeper, richer human life, a more total entrance into the mystery of God working its way out in human lives. We can translate all the language of the social scientists into a spiritual, religious transition:

> The spirituality of mid-life flows from the tasks of mid-life, characterized in Jungian terms as inwardness, individuation, self-realization, integration, reconciliation, coming to selfhood.[7]

Like Peter we grow into adult maturity by giving up what we have for what we do not yet have on the word of someone who loves us. Like a swinger on some cosmic trapeze, we let go of one bar before the other has quite swung to us and, with our feet firmly planted in mid-air, we trust in the love we have known, and wait for the new life to come.

> I believe that in this psychological turmoil grace is working gently, is painfully . . . inviting our true selves to emerge from the womb into the fulness of life. Quite often the whole process of middle age crisis is nothing less than a mystical experience of death and resurrection to a new life which is filled with true joy.[8]

This is the invitation. Obviously, from all that has gone on before, we do not accept that invitation lightly, and the passage will not be easy. As Brennan and Brewi point out, this search through soul-sized affairs, this enterprise of exploration into God, will take each of us in crisis through our whole selves, as we re-evaluate and choose our whole lives, seeking to discover the deepest ultimate meaning about ourselves.[9]

In the following section, as a more structured way to view this mid-life transition as a faith experience, we want to look more carefully at a final model of religious interpretation. James Fowler's *Stages of Faith* looks at the entire spectrum of life as a gradual growth in trust in whatever one calls God. His work is especially illuminative for those in middle years.

Notes

1. Gerard Manley Hopkins, "Thou art indeed just, Lord, if I contend with Thee," from *A Hopkins Reader* (Image Books: Garden City, N.Y., 1966) p. 82.

2. The biblical text used for this treatment of Lamentations is the Revised Standard Version.

3. Hopkins, *op. cit.,* p. 76.

4. John Shea, "Prayer for the Long Haul," from *The Hour of the Unexpected* (Argus: Niles, Ill., 1977) p. 104.

5. Thomas Merton, "Whether There is Enjoyment in Bitterness," from *The Strange Islands* (New York: New Directions Books, 1957) pp. 25–26.

6. William Kraft, from *Review for Religious,* Vol. 37, November 1978, p. 873.

7. Janice Brewi and Anne Brennan, *Mid-Life: Psychological and Spiritual Perspectives* (Crossroad: New York, 1982) p. 50.

8. William Johnston, *The Inner Eye of Love* (Harper and Row: New York, 1978) p. 148.

9. Brewi and Brennan, *op. cit.,* p. 33.

2

The Stages of Faith of James Fowler

The groundbreaking work of James Fowler presents six stages of faith development. Based on interviews with hundreds of persons of various faith traditions, as well as agnostics and atheists, Fowler describes *faith* as a *verb*, an active, constructive, interpretive mode of being. As opposed to any specific belief *system*, or content, or some *thing* known, faith, for Fowler is a way of knowing and interpreting our experience. Faith gives life meaning or purpose—allows us to move into the future. Faith is "trust in another, and loyalty to a transcendent center of value and power."[1]

Fowler is careful to point out that not all persons go through all stages. We can fixate and cease to grow at any of them. Each stage, however, must follow in sequence; we cannot skip steps. Also we may find ourselves straddling two stages during a period of transition. The transition from one stage to another is precipitated by the inability to apply former solutions to new problems or questions. Thus, moving from one stage to another constitutes a kind of death and resurrection, more painful and yet more life-giving at each successive level.

These stages of faith are more descriptive than prescriptive. That is, stage development does not point to a level where all people "should" be. Fowler maintains there is a kind of grace or integrity when any stage is fully lived.

The crucial point to be grasped is that the image of human completion or wholeness offered by faith development theory is not an estate to be attained or a stage to be realized. Rather, it is a way of being and moving, a way of being on pilgrimage.[2]

Thus, we have canonized people in the Roman Church for perfectly keeping a religious "rule," even though following laws seems to be a "lesser" stage of faith development. In truth, we can be truly holy and integral at any stage, living perfectly and consistently our understanding of God's invitation and our response.

Development is not a result of education, but rather comes out of engagement with the givenness and crises of daily life. Fowler is also hesitant to assign a chronological age to the various stages; many adults remain forever in preliminary stages of the development of their faith.

To describe most simply the faith progress would be to say that we move from an initial world/faith view in stage one that is primarily ego-centric (comparable to the world view of a small child turned in upon itself), to a world view that reflects the significance of belonging to a broadening social group (as in Jung's task for young adulthood). Finally, we move to a larger world-view that transcends the boundaries of specific groups or ideologies. This dynamic involves a painful process of surrendering control and certitude (comparable to Jung's task for middle adulthood).[3] Let us look more carefully at stages three, four, and five, for it is here that our understanding of the mid-life transition is especially enriched.

Stage Three

Fowler's stage three, enigmatically termed "synthetic conventional," is reached anywhere from adolescence to middle-age or even beyond. Fowler maintains that most church-goers never move beyond stage three. This fact helps to explain much of the painful polarization within the communities of all our faith traditions.

A person in stage three tends to be conformist, relying heavily on others' expectations and judgments whether that "other" be boss, spouse, church, or any other "authority." The stage three person has not fully achieved what Erikson calls the *identity* which allows for an independent perspective.

In stage three, a personal myth about who one is in relation to the past and the future begins to emerge; one can describe oneself through stories, through models of behavior from faith traditions or elsewhere.

As an advance over the previous stage, a person in stage three has a new ability to trust in oneself, but only insofar as he or she chooses competent *outside authorities*. *Law* is extremely important, whether church, civic or societal, for authority is in every case external.

Stage three is characterized by a personal sense of God's presence (the surety of an expression like, "Jesus is my personal savior," would be frequent in this stage). This faith, however, is coupled with an inability to evaluate or step outside one's own religious belief system. Religious tradition or ideological stance tends to be an unexamined but dearly held "given."

Previously in stage two, a person was inclined to have a rather strong belief in "earning merit," or winning the divine favor as one measures up to religious expectations. Similarly, stage two emphasized "reciprocity," or a faith in which God rewards us as we deserve. If we "play ball with God, God will play ball with us." These convictions of *merit* and *reciprocity* often continue in stage three as a residue.

Also in the third stage, *symbols* of the sacred tend to take on the characteristics of the sacred itself, without reflection or distinction. What parish has not experienced the turmoil of parishioners when a statue is removed, or the American flag is taken from the sanctuary, or a tabernacle is placed in a prayer-chapel elsewhere in the church than on the main altar? Symbols take on a sacredness of their own, with a meaning that cannot be easily questioned or altered. For people in stage three, to change the symbol is to disrespect the essence of the symbol.

Finally, a stage three person's interpersonal relationships provide the construct for looking at any larger pictures. For example, one may commiserate with a black or Hispanic friend who is out of work, but find it difficult to see institutions or socio-political structures that contribute to an oppressive situation of which a suffering friend is only a part. The person in this third stage finds it difficult if not impossible to abstract or to universalize on religious or moral issues.

A transition from stage three to stage four can be precipitated by the recognition of contradictory opinions held by equally respected authorities, forcing one into a significant personal decision. For many Roman Catholics, this transition began following the Second Vatican Council when authority itself called for a re-evaluation and renewal of church practice, ritual, and parish life. Any experience that forces one to broaden perspective and inspect attitudes could provide the catalyst for this transition—e.g., entrance into the army, attending graduate school, joining the Peace Corps, an immersion experience in a third or fourth world country or in an inner-city ghetto, or the sudden unexpected death of a loved one—any change that forces one out of a too-narrowly-constructed world-view.

Stage Four

Whatever the precipitating crisis or experience, the individual in stage four, which Fowler calls "individuative/reflexive," begins to reveal greater autonomy and integrity, gradually assuming personal responsibility for commitments, decisions, and faith. Reliance on exterior sources decreases considerably, although support from significant others remains very helpful and important.

The awakening of the "executive ego" now allows for enough distance from a belief system, or church, or parents to enable the individual to evaluate and perhaps demythologize. The belief system previously tacitly accepted becomes explicit. In this process the person in this fourth stage tends to adopt a dichotomizing, either/or mentality, and to evince a certain self-righteousness about newly conceived attitudes or values.

To illustrate this, Fowler tells an anecdote about cultural-analyst Harvey Cox who, in his youth, attended a Catholic midnight Mass with a young woman: "As Mass climaxed and the people were receiving Eucharist," Harvey said, "his college-aged girl friend, who had just completed Anthropology 101, turned to him and whispered, 'That's just a primitive totemic ritual, you know.' "[4]

A person in stage four can appear rebellious and counter-dependent. Parents or teachers are denigrated for not adequately living up to the person's newly discovered ideals. When this transition occurs in mid-life, the struggle is even more traumatic as we separate identity from church, or spouse, or work-place.

In stage four, an interpersonal perspective gives way to a broader awareness of social systems and institutions. An individual begins to see beyond the reality of this city, or country, this woman, or this homosexual, or this native American, to develop a critical sense toward impersonal imperatives of law, rules, and standards that govern social positions and possibilities.

In opening up to a much broader world, the stage four person's consciousness obviously embraces severe tensions: individual needs vs. community or family, relative vs. absolute, and so forth. Sometimes maintaining these tensions becomes too difficult and the balance collapses in one direction or another. The person exaggerates either an unreal dependence on self, or complete subordination to another. Regarding subordination, some young adults opt for an ideologically grounded community whose leader offers secure solutions and answers. Cults provide an apt example of this, whether they be inside or outside a personal faith tradition (e.g., some charismatic renewal, or Hari-Krishna).

In a kind of desperation, some people simply regress to the comfort of a previous stage in which there is less ambiguity, or else they sustain a kind of precarious "holding pattern," balancing intellectual perceptions and behavior from the previous stage. Obviously, the transition from stage three to stage four is a protracted affair with a good bit of going back and forth, particularly in times of crisis. Generally, a move to stage five (paradoxical/consolidative) is precipitated by the emergence of the unconscious, and feelings of restlessness and disillusionment with one's life in spite of achieving personal goals. "Is that all there is?" An inner demand for deeper integrity and transparency asserts itself.

Stage Five

For those in mid-life transition, the move from stage four to stage five is most significant. This faith development presupposes the life experience of failure, disillusionment, suffering, most often associated with mid-life. Such experiences provide a wide-angled lens with which to view reality. Fowler insists that none of those he interviewed evidenced a movement into stage five before the age of thirty-five, and most were older. Our experience would indicate that one's personal history is a key factor here.

If the stage four person tended to be "either/or" in judgments, the stage five person sees and is able to be sympathetic to both sides of a question. With a growing ability to live with ambiguity, the stage five person can identify both with the stage three persons who threaten to leave the church if the altar rail is removed, *and* with the stage four individual who offers the same response if it is not removed. Stage five, then, is characterized by an ability to live with polarity, and to experience compassion for people maintaining opposite extremes.

One sees the interrelatedness of things in a kind of dialogical knowing. As Fowler writes: "The emergence of stage five is something like realizing that the behavior of light requires that it be understood *both* as a wave phenomenon *and* in particles of energy."[5]

Jung's task at mid-life involved the invitation to come to terms with the fact that the conscious ego is not the master of its own house. This is expressed in the way one approaches life—more receptively, less aggressively. The consolidation of ego strength in stage four, by establishing an explicit ideological system with a firm delineation of one's perceived identity, gives way in stage five to an openness to the emerging unconscious parts of oneself.

Alive to paradox and the truth of apparent polarities (young/old, creation/destruction, prayer/action) and contradictions, the stage five person maintains and appreciates the tensions of life, establishing a tenuous but authentically creative equilibrium. The stage three person could not risk looking beyond a firmly established value and faith tradition. The stage four person perhaps exaggerated his or her critique of that same tradition. The stage five person moves beyond disillusionment to the very heart of his or her faith tradition, while appreciating the beauty and commonality of all roads to God. Fowler contends that no one reaches or remains at a stage five development outside of some faith tradition which can now be both accepted *and* critically evaluated.

In stage five, one's compassion and interest reach out not just to prominent individuals in one's personal history, but to all the people of the world who are members of a single human family. One is open to those who are "other," or, more accurately, one begins to realize that no one is "other." Thus, one becomes, in Erikson's terms, *generative*, willing to risk enabling and empowering others out of honest concern and love for them.

In summary, then, this description of James Fowler's stages helps us to understand the mid-life passage:

At stage three everything is clear, ordered. "God's in his heaven, all's right with the world." We are in control, and so is our religious response. The good are rewarded: the wicked are punished. If we follow the law, obey the rules, everything will turn out just fine.

Then something happens to challenge this interpretation of life; often it does not happen until early middle-age. If we accept the challenge and do not run away, we begin to move into stage four.

Here we enter into autonomy, independence. We are still in control, are uneasy with other opposing stances, and perhaps intolerant of those in stage three from which we have just come. Although autonomous, we are somewhat self-centered, and uncomfortable with the unclear, the ambiguous.

Again, something happens that disturbs our worldview, our certitude, our ability to hold on to answers and control. This transition from stage four to stage five seems to us to most commonly mark the discomfort of the mid-life transition. It is at this time that we must become capable of coping with the ambiguity of life, capable of living with tension (neither young nor old, neither male nor female, neither creative nor destructive, neither alone nor separate, but a bit of each). Then we can begin to live in a world we cannot control, and trust the operation of this world to a compassionate God. Every stage demands a kind of dying and rising, but this death and new life demands the most traumatic change of all, for it requires a total change of our view of the world, ourselves, others, and the Divine.

Notes

1. James Fowler, *Stages of Faith* (Harper and Row, San Francisco, Calif., 1981) p. 14. Throughout these pages we rely generally on the work of Fowler as we briefly explain his theory. Again, no effort is made to identify the exact page reference for each informational item.

2. James Fowler, *Becoming Adult, Becoming Christian* (San Francisco: Harper and Row, 1984) p. 74.

3. Sheila M. Murphy, *Midlife Wanderer* (Whitinsville, Mass.: Affirmation Books, 1983) p. 59.

4. Fowler, *Stages of Faith,* p. 181.

5. *Ibid.,* p. 184.

PART III

The Pieces of Our Brokenness

Introduction

Throughout these pages we have consistently compared the mid-life transition to that of childbirth, new birth, third birth, in which we are mother to ourselves; the struggle and the pain of this birth-giving is our own. In this section we will look more carefully at some of the pangs of this birth, some of the pieces of our brokenness, seeing each pain as part of the possibility of new life, new creation.

In earlier chapters we offered a variety of ways to view this mid-life transition, to give a name to the pain, offer words with which to talk about the struggle. Whether we speak of the transition in terms of Fowler's movement from stage four to stage five, or Jung's individuation, or Gilligan's recognition of the need for women to care for themselves as well as for others—whatever model we use—all imply the ability to live imperfectly in an imperfect world. To be adult, to successfully survive the mid-life transition, and to accomplish this new birth requires a growing ability to live with ambiguity, tension, polarity, and through trial to become more fully free. We are invited over and over again to steadfastly refuse escaping the struggle.

Throughout this section, we will rely on one of our previous models, at least in outline. We will suggest that Levinson's polarities give rise to four central struggles at mid-life. Each of these struggles, while part of the entire gamut of human life, becomes particularly acute now. Each involves a particular issue, a kind of chaos, that needs to be resolved at mid-life, and each provides the possibility for new birth, new creation.

We live in a tension between being young and old. If we become prematurely old, we remain once-born, and die long before our body does. If we try to remain young, refuse to admit our limits, stay external rather than internal, we risk the particular malady of mid-life we call BURN-OUT.

We live in a tension between the destructive and creative dimensions of our past, and of ourselves now. We realize that we are capable of and have perpetrated much damage to ourselves and to others. We need to assimilate our own imperfections and that of the universe. On one side of the tension we risk naiveté, perpetual adolescence and causing ever more harm, oblivious of our destructive capabilities. On the other side, facing our inadequacies, we risk discouragement, even real or metaphorical suicide; we wrestle with the reality of DEPRESSION.

We live in a tension between attachment and separation. We need to balance whichever has been emphasized in the first part of life with a need in the middle of life to search for inner spaces. We face head-on the temptation to pour ourselves out in an external world, trying to give from an empty cup; if we enter into that inner world, we face LONELINESS in a profound and more ominous degree than we had previously imagined.

Finally, we live in a tension between male and female, the *animus* and *anima* fighting for recognition in the consciousness of each of us. This raises in new ways all the issues of SEXUALITY and INTIMACY in human life.

Obviously, each of these four pieces of our brokenness (BURN-OUT, DEPRESSION, LONELINESS, SEXUALITY/INTIMACY) cuts through all polarities and tensions of mid-life. We will consider them in turn, not so much offering solutions to enduring human realities, but suggesting ways to consider them. We also hope to give a language to talk about them.

1

Burn-Out

The sight of a familiar home burned to the ground or a forest ravaged by fire is not unlike people we frequently see, depleted of energy and therefore of their physical and mental resources, hollow images of a former, vibrant self. One woman described to us why she had resigned her professional ministry in mid-year: "I'm exhausted, impatient with my kids, finding myself unable to concentrate to make decisions. I haven't slept well or been able to pray for months, and have had the same cold for weeks. I have nothing left." A deeply reflective person, she had the good sense to step out of her impossible situation, but the ultimate cure is beyond even this step.

Others, determined to prove they can still meet their own or others' expectations, continue to push themselves into a state of numbness or a feeling of interior deadness and depression which moves into cynicism, withdrawal, a deep sense of being unappreciated. Sour on themselves, overwhelmed with irritability and bitterness, they resent the very people they love, or the people they want to minister to. The person who experiences this advanced burn-out is not, on the surface, a very pleasant figure.

What causes this unnecessary phenomenon that threatens one's life-style, professional competence, and entire well-being?

The frantic pace at which our culture moves certainly provides one factor:

At the turn of this century, for instance, the major cause
of death was infectious disease, and among the most
prevalent psychological afflictions was hysteria, a condition in which there is some marked physical impair-
ment—such as the inability to lift an arm—with no
physical cause. Today infectious disease as a cause of
death, in industrialized nations at least, has been re-
placed by heart disease, arteriosclerosis, and cancer,
while in the psychological realm one hardly ever encounters a case of hysteria. Instead we hear of condi-
tions such as burnout, and this reflects the changing
condition of human life. [1]

Though burn-out is not just a mid-life affliction, it certainly affects many at this time. The primary cause of burn-
out is that one excessively strives to meet unreal expectations imposed by oneself or by others. As we get older, the
sheer physical extertion needed to keep up our hectic pace
is impossible. Like Alice in *Through the Looking Glass*, we
find that it takes all the running we can do just to keep in
the same place. Whenever our expectation level for ourselves and/or others (children, spouse, students, patients,
parishioners) stands in dramatic opposition to reality, and
we persist in these expectations, trouble brews.

If we refer back to Jung's personality model, we recall
that the *persona* or "public face" is largely molded by the
expectations of others or unreal expectations of my own.
The *persona* adopted in youth is simply no longer acceptable in the middle of life. At mid-life, some resist obvious
physical changes accompanying the aging process and seek
to prove the contrary. They force body, mind, and spirit to
meet the ego's expectations and prove nature wrong. They
refuse to admit their authentic, emerging self. This causes

a tremendous amount of stress, and hence, the many signs of burn-out.

Not every personality is susceptible to burn-out. Usually this phenomenon is limited to rather dynamic, goal-oriented persons who tend to be perfectionistic and idealistic. These are often private persons, reluctant to share, whose goals are not personally determined, but adopted from others, and, to a larger or lesser degree, externally imposed. Frantic work to maintain one's adopted or conscious image rather than one's real and unique personality forces the phenomenon of burn-out.

Ironically, authentic workaholics seldom burn out. Their compulsive work is a defense mechanism against emotional involvement or intimacy with people, and they do not suffer the same consequences as the idealistic dynamic types. They have their own pathology.

Psychologist Dr. Herbert Freudenberger suggests a practical exercise to help one be more aware of inappropriate gaps between the adopted ego image and the emerging self:[2]

1. Think about your image, that competent *you* others have come to expect so much of . . . think about your schedule, the tasks you perform, your family's expectations, your own expectations of yourself. Write a short vignette of the *you* the world sees and hears every day.

2. Put that aside, close your eyes, and let the real *you* emerge . . . the one you see first thing in the morning when you walk into the bathroom, the one you meet when you are by yourself. Let the real *you* speak, express feelings, needs, hopes, fears.

3. Compare the two and see how wide the gap is. No one else can effectively point out your inner conflicts. You have to be willing to look at yourself honestly and deeply.

4. Later, tell someone you trust something you learned about yourself ("I'm really tired," or "I'm eating, . . . drinking, . . . smoking too much," or "I'm not getting enough time to myself").

Mid-life is a time for greater ego-passivity when the unconscious begins to emerge, replenishing psychic energy exhausted by the demands of the ego. We only have so much psychic energy; it needs to be restored if we are to remain integrated, healthy persons.

John Sanford suggests the image of a mountain lake for the store of psychic energy.[3] Just as a lake needs both an outlet for its water and one or more inlets so fresh water can come in, so does our human psyche. For most of us, the equivalent of the outgoing stream is the flow of energy expended in work, play, and interpersonal relationships. Like the lake, we also need sources of energy, inlets of renewed strength, in order to maintain a balance. And it is here that the balance often breaks down.

We need to turn to sources of renewed energy: creative, intimate relationships, physical exercise, journaling, prayer or solitude (people who burn out seldom take time to be alone), dreams, or any use of creative imagination in fantasizing anew, or amplifying a recent dream (our fantasy life can tell us what our spirit or our body wants and needs).

Communication is perhaps the most important aspect of renewing energy. This communication can consist of pleasant mutual affirmation with a good friend or the sharing of one's faith story with another. Honest communication may also involve resolving conflict, for unresolved conflict drains our psychic energy. The husband or wife who refuses to discuss a problem buries the anger, but anger is never buried alive and it struggles underneath our immediate awareness, draining us of energy and life.

When we recognize our inability to produce or cope, we

are often tempted to intensify what has caused the stress in the first place ("I'll just try harder"), or we may turn to alcohol, drugs, sex, or some other escape as a way to energize ourselves. As an all-or-nothing person, susceptible to burnout, we may even abuse legitimate physical exercise ("If two miles are good, why not six?"). These tend to be dead-end solutions.

Self-knowledge and faith are perhaps most important for prevention or recovery from burn-out. The secret of recapturing energy lies in awareness of our authentic self, our feelings, needs, desires. Faith is likewise a key factor for recovery. Possibly "God's work" has become more important than God. There is an element of blindness in every case of burn-out. Faith teaches us that ultimately hope is in God, not in things, situations, or even other people. Faith gives us a sense of who really is doing the work, the loving, the ministering—eliminating from us any messianic complex we may hold onto. In this way, burn-out can become not just a painful state of disillusionment, but may provide the possibility for dramatic growth in faith.

Notes

1. Sanford, *Ministry Burnout*, *op. cit.*, p. 3.
2. Dr. Herbert J. Freudenberger, *Burn-Out* (Bantam Books: New York, 1980) pp. 27ff.
3. *Ministry Burnout*, *op. cit.*, p. 104.

2

Depression

"Depression has been called the world's number one public health problem. In fact, it is so widespread it is considered the common cold of psychiatric disturbance."[1] Depression frequently stalks the trail of those at mid-life.

We hasten to point out that not all "low moods" are depression. Loneliness is not depression, nor is the feeling of disappointment. A person acutely disappointed will regain a sense of hope when the situation changes. One with the "blues" can often be cheered at the prospect of good company or a change of pace.

Persons grieving or mourning the death of a loved one, the break-up of a marriage, or the loss of a friendship manifest many of the symptoms of depression, but there are differences. A specific event triggers a person's grief. Normally mourners do not lose the ability to continue functioning, although perhaps they proceed at a mitigated pace. Moreover, depending on the personality of the individual and the magnitude of the specific loss, the most intense signs of grieving gradually wane and the feelings of sadness and loss lessen. This is always an individual process, however. We do not grieve on a specific time schedule and we grieve at successively different levels of our being.

Depression can be the result of physical problems such as hormonal disturbance in the endocrine functioning or a condition related to low blood sugar. In these instances, the underlying organic cause of the depression can be treated by medication and/or diet. The depression we primarily speak of refers to disturbance in our emotional lives.

To understand the difference between this latter type of depression and low moods, let us compare the person to a violin.

> When the strings are properly tuned they vibrate and emit sound. One can then play a glad or sad song, a dirge or an ode to joy. If the strings are improperly tuned, the result will be cacophony. If they are flaccid and without tone, you will get no sound at all. The instrument will be "dead," unable to respond. That is the condition of the depressed person; he or she is unable to respond.[2]

Normally the gamut of feeling a person expresses indicates the breadth of the personality. In a healthy individual, feelings constantly change—from anger to love, sadness or joy. Each feeling indicates the individual's personal response to the environment. Each directly expresses the life forces within the person. This is precisely what the depressed person is unable to do: express feeling. Depression represents the absence of emotion, a lack of responsiveness; therefore, it is not actual feeling, but rather an inability to feel. In the technical sense, one does not "feel" depressed.[3]

Like the burned-out person, a candidate for depression sets, or allows others to set, unreal expectations or goals for himself or herself. By and large, the depressed person is more emotionally dependent on others for approval, leading a life frequently governed by "shoulds" and "oughts."

In one sense, the goals established are not necessarily unreal in themselves; the reward supposedly to follow from their achievement is. In other words, what is essentially sought is not so much the goal as such (success in business or ministry, a higher degree, the perfect marriage, writing a book), but a sense of self-worth and esteem expected to follow on the fulfilling of the goal. Thus, even a man who sells his business at a considerable profit or the professional woman who achieves a sought-for position might still be plunged into depression. Of course this is obviously true for the person who fails to meet goals. When I fail to live up to my idealized expectations of who I am (idealized self) or even when I do live up to them, I fail to derive a basic sense of self-acceptance. The point is, if I am not in touch with my authentic self, I have to prove that I am someone I am not. I need not waste energy chasing after an idealized self but to come to terms with the person I really am.

When I realize my inability to achieve peace and satisfaction, I experience rage, self-hatred, anxiety, helplessness, impotence and guilt. In an attempt to keep these feelings from tearing me apart, I *de-press* them. The problem is, once I de-press a feeling—it hardly matters which one—all of my affective level shuts down. Like throwing a master switch, I cannot turn off just one part of my emotional life without affecting the rest. This accounts for the sense of numbness and the inability to respond.

Most of us experience the "garden variety" of depression, rather than a more serious clinical type. I have a sense of "dragging," or experiencing the "blahs." Fatigue, in spite of sufficient sleep, loss of interest in my circle of work, friends, community or family, feelings of inferiority and inadequacy, outbursts of temper or a sort of smoldering resentment or self-pity—all indicate depression. I may be sleeping too little (doing three loads of wash during the course of the night) or too much (nine hours plus naps).

Generally, somatic disorders such as backaches, headaches, chronic colds, and gastrointestinal difficulties accompany depression. Any kind of growing dependence on alcohol or other stimulants, or sedatives, provides a tip-off.

Forms of compulsiveness—working, eating, smoking—can be expressions of the anxiety that accompanies depression. The important thing is to check my present behavior with my normal behavior. If, in spite of the presence of some of the above symptoms, I function well, I am not clinically depressed.

At mid-life, I am called to greater interiority and to a recognition of my deeper identity based not on "should" and "ought" but on the freedom of the daughters and sons of God. The idealized image formed by the ego puts up strong resistance in order to maintain control and to keep the personality "in line." Mid-life tasks (such as accepting a growing awareness of my vulnerability and inability to control, owning parts of my personality that I dislike, or resolving painful unfinished business of the past) can foster a collapse of illusions about myself. Depressive reactions can flow out of this type of disillusioning process.

On the other hand, at mid-life it is normal to mourn or grieve over the aging of the body and the decline in energy, the loss of earlier relationships, and the impossibility of fulfilling all of my desires because of previous decisions.

It seems to us that the fact women are much more prone to depression stems, in large part, from what our culture constantly plays back to them. They are "other" than the norm of white American males and therefore deficient. The cultural roots of depression among women center around learned helplessness and a position of self-effacement which are often applauded.[4] It is particularly difficult for many women to deal effectively and positively with key mid-life tasks until they recognize and reject that oppressiveness.

The more I know and pursue my own deepest desires, and take responsibility for actions flowing from them, the sooner the depression will disappear. Usually when I experience depression, I need to be more independent of approval from others and more trusting in God and self.

One of many helpful approaches in dealing with midlife depression is *cognitive therapy,* a technique developed by Dr. Aaron Beck of the University of Pennsylvania School of Medicine. He posits that the way I structure experience by my thinking determines the quality and appropriateness of affective responses. In other words, I can skew my perceptions of reality by way of what he calls "cognitive distortions."[5]

Examples of such cognitive distortions are:

overgeneralization ("This always happens to me!").
focusing on the negative (out of a very positive evaluation you focus in on the one area mentioned for improvement).
jumping to conclusions (an exhausted student falls asleep and you conclude the entire class is bored).
emotional reasoning ("I *feel* inadequate to the project; therefore others must perceive me in the same way").
assuming responsibility in areas that are not mine (when a child comes home with a poor report card the parent decides: "I must be a poor parent").

Such cognitive distortions represent ordinary and consistent filters that fuel the lack of self-esteem, as I underestimate my abilities, and tend to blame myself unduly.

Besides eliminating cognitive disorders, or learning to think about ourselves in a new way, we also suggest other helps to deal constructively with depression. Some are obvious in light of what we have said: physical exercise, externalizing the anger by journaling or physical expression (beating a pillow), talking to a trusted other, forming realistic personally-determined goals, exploring conflicts that have triggered depression, utilizing fantasies to learn about one's deepest desires.

Less obvious, perhaps, but more significant, we need to act contrary to the depression. Assertiveness and depression are closely related. One of the most effective ways of dealing with low self-esteem and its resultant depression is assertive behavior.

It is also helpful to be gentle and loving to myself by indulging in simple pleasures and rewards such as getting my hair styled, going fishing, reading a novel, enjoying a good dinner, taking a long warm bath.

Finally, solitude is imperative. Many fear solitude because they equate it with loneliness but the two are quite different. Those who flee solitude miss discovering themselves and God. It is interesting to observe that those who really take time for solitude become less dependent on others, a firm step in the right direction for overcoming depression.

Above all, I must be loved by the Lord in prayer, hear the encouragement of close friends, and pay simple attention to the genuine giftedness of daily life.

Notes

1. David Burns, *Feeling Good* (New York: Signet Books, 1980) p. 9.

2. Alexander Lowen, *Depression and the Body* (New York: Penguin Books, 1980) p. 18.

3. Lowen, *ibid.,* p. 78.

4. Helen De Rosis and V. Pellegrino, *The Book of Hope: How Women Can Overcome Depression* (New York: Bantam Books, 1981) p. 3.

5. Burns, *op. cit.,* pp. 31ff.

3

Loneliness

A splendid poster reminds us of a central truth at the heart of the human experience of loneliness. A father holds his daughter on his shoulders as they gaze together at a vast ocean. Beneath the picture are the words: "We ask God for answers and God sends us a person to help us live with the questions." That person, finally, is Jesus, but God also comes to us incarnate in many others. We are not alone, but each of us often feels that way. As we wrestle with the tensions between our need to be with others and our need to be alone, especially in the middle of our lives, we will feel acutely that deep and existential loneliness that is so much a part of the human condition.

We want to remember that Jesus, the Word enfleshed among us, shared with us that loneliness. He begins his public life deliberately entering into that solitude so necessary for human integration: "Then Jesus was led by the Spirit out into the wilderness to be tempted" (Mt 4:1). He endured the loneliness of being misunderstood by everyone, even those closest to him: "Do you not yet understand?" (Mt 16:9). Before his darkest hour he is personally and psychologically abandoned by his friends and feels that isolation deeply: "So you had not the strength to keep awake with me one hour?" (Mt 26:40). And in his final moments he experiences the deepest human abandonment, the sense of being estranged even from his God: "My God, my God, why have you deserted me?" (Mt 27:47).

So we Christians radically are not alone when we approach the issue of human loneliness. And we recognize that part of the human experience is that we do not have here a lasting city, that we will never be completely at home in this life. Part of us longs for, waits for, is restless for another, as Augustine's famous line reminds us: "Our hearts are restless, Lord, and they will not rest until they rest in thee."

Still, granted that Jesus has gone before us with the same experience, and we know that some experience of loneliness is unavoidable, still we want to better understand this universal but unique experience and want to know more clearly how to cope with it.

Perhaps we first need a rather simple explanation, realizing that all simple explanations run the risk of being simplistic. It seems to us that there is really only one human problem which all human beings share in various degrees of intensity. All of us know and are bothered by the absolutely universal human experience that "I am not loving, or loved enough." We may emphasize the first or second part of that statement, may forget the feelings for some stretch of time, may experience this reality in various degrees of discomfort, but, finally, when we are troubled, it is this reality that troubles us—our inability, our failure to love or be loved enough!

In order to cope with this pervasive human experience, we take two radically different life-approaches. Some of us *inflate*. We charge; we stay terribly busy so that no one, including ourselves, will notice. The inflater (who is, parenthetically, prone to burn-out), rushing hither and yon in a million directions, responding to a crowded schedule and a too-packed agenda, stays always a little bit angry because everyone expects so much of him or her. So much is asked, so much remains to be done, there is so little time, so many demands, so little help. This anger stays on the surface, however. Underneath, the inflater knows the schedule has been personally created. The truly dominant emotion is *fear*. The inflater knows that to stop this hectic pace is to risk letting oneself and the world know the shallowness beneath. The fear hovers constantly over the inflater's head, beneath the inflater's heart, reminding him or her that "you are not loving or loved enough."

Others learn to cope with the inability or failure to be loving or loved enough by *deflating,* withdrawing, staying on the edge, being careful, aloof, alone, apart. The deflater (who is, parenthetically again, more prone to depression) always appears to be *afraid*. This fear, like the inflater's anger, is on the surface, however. Deflaters look afraid—stand on the edge of the crowd, keep to themselves. But underneath the fear the deflaters' dominant emotion is *anger,* for it is not fair to be loved so partially, so poorly and to be so unable to love in return.

As we have said so often, the coping mechanisms learned in the first part of our lives seem to break down somewhere in our middle-years. The inflater no longer has the energy, the drive, the "strokes" needed to continue the charge into life. The deflater is forced by circumstances of simple human need to earn a living, raise a family, cope with life, to enter in and take part. The bubble bursts and the loneliness, only half-noticed before, breaks fully bloomed into the experience of the mid-life person.

Generally, because it has been part of the deflater's experience all along, the one who has coped by withdrawing will experience mid-life loneliness with less disturbance. He or she has had to deal with being alone before, so the emptiness felt now is not entirely new. But the inflater, the one who has attacked life, stayed busy, built empires and personal shrines, walls of isolation and protection, will perhaps find this stopping, this being quiet, excruciatingly lonely and unbearable.

Eventually, this experience of not being loved or loving enough needs to be embraced. And this embrace is the beginning of salvation, for real redemption lies in recognizing that "what proves that God loves us is that Christ died for us while we were still sinners" (Rom 5:8–9). We do not have to be perfect to be loved, do not have to respond adequately to be saved, and this recognition ultimately pulls us out of our loneliness, for, on the deepest level, we *are* loved enough, loved infinitely, eternally. Obviously, then, loneliness is a religious issue, a faith question.

Our initial remarks, however true, are perhaps too simple; we need to look more carefully at the variety of experiences of loneliness, especially those that pertain more specifically to mid-life. Ronald Rolheiser, in his fine book *The Loneliness Factor,*[1] suggests five different kinds of loneliness, three of which are especially pertinent to our subject.

Rolheiser speaks initially of *alienation loneliness* which endures in some forms throughout life—the experience of being "other than," apart from the crowd, the abused child, the fat kid, the last chosen, the elderly, the black, the woman, the foreigner. Alienation is experienced by some always, and by all sometimes when we know "I do not belong here," or "I am not at home here." We experience it even in church: we have all been there. Alienation flows out of our defensiveness and human cruelty to one another.

Rolheiser's second kind of loneliness is more frequently problematic at mid-life. *Restlessness loneliness,* somewhat like Peggy Lee's lament "Is that all there is?" or more profoundly Augustine's "restless till we rest in thee," grows out of the human reality that *unlimited* desires are always met with *limited* fulfillment. This universal human experience seems necessary if we are to be alive and conscious. Still, it is often not until mid-life that restlessness becomes unavoidable, acute. Our parents and/or our friends die, and we face our own mortality. Our business life has peaked and we have nowhere to go but down, or sideways in some lateral arabesque. Our physical powers diminish. Our children disappoint us. Our church is less a sign of Christ's presence than we had ever dreamed. We are deeply and ineluctably disappointed in life, experiencing the loneliness, the restlessness of the misplaced, the ungrounded, the disappointed. On the one hand, insofar as this loneliness flows out of the reality of sin in ourselves and in our world, it is an unhealthy reality that needs to be corrected. On the other hand, insofar as this restlessness results from the human condition, it needs to be healthily faced and accepted. Discerning which is which constitutes a major mid-life task to which we will return in a moment.

The third type of loneliness suggested by Rolheiser is *fantasy loneliness*. This results from a lack of contact with "truth," as we build up unrealistic expectations. In extreme forms it is the loneliness of a kid on drugs who goes straight, an alcoholic when dry, or a workaholic when not busy: the fantasy created by false living no longer works, and we are left feeling disjointed, discomforted. If we create a false world, we will be disappointed in the real one and experience loneliness. The same loneliness occurs when the prince never does come to kiss sleeping beauty awake, the knight in shining armor never arrives to make a boring life bearable, the magic goes out of a mirage marriage, or any other relationship, the beauty with which we began becomes wrinkled and gray. So often in mid-life we are forced to accept the unreality of our fantasies and live in the world as it is and not as we would want it to be. This surrendering of fantasies creates a lonely time, a time between what is real and what we longed for. Everyone in mid-life must necessarily enter into this fantasy loneliness, for each of us must face that neither we nor the world will be all that we expected. The degree of fantasy which we allowed to frame our earlier life will dictate the degree of this experience of loneliness we undergo.

Though it is again a part of life, we experience Rolheiser's fourth type of loneliness, *rootlessness loneliness*, most intensely at mid-life. This rootlessness describes the experience of having whatever we rooted our lives in disturbed, challenged, or pulled out from under us completely. All are affected by *Future Shock* and rapid change. Very little is permanent, from paper plates to serial marriages. We live in a Kleenex society, using things and people and throwing them away. Life cannot be lived without roots, absolutes, security, tradition. Many, at mid-life, are forced for a variety of reasons to examine their absolutes, sometimes to divorce their traditions, especially if they are another's thrust upon us. Recent psychological studies indicate that there is a degree of change or stress created by that change that any human person can withstand—everyone has a breaking point, beyond which change becomes destructive. More change occurs at mid-life than perhaps at any time after childhood, as family ties, religious certitudes, moral values, ideals, heroes, institutions all seem to fail us, or, at least, to demand re-examination.

The religious implications of this loneliness, this rootlessness experienced at mid-life, loom incredibly significant, for the reality finally faced is that we can only live fully human lives with something that is not ultimately relative, something (Someone?) that perdures through whatever other changes occur. If we have not done so previously, we need to ask the ultimate questions and seek the ultimate answers to the meaning of human life, our relationship with the universe, and with God. When we are forced to recognize that everyone will die, that there is nothing and no one on whom we can absolutely rely in this life, and that we are ultimately able to be rooted only in God, a life of true faith becomes not only possible, but necessary to escape from this rootlessness.

Finally, Rolheiser mentions *blues loneliness,* that sort of "rainy days and Mondays always make me blue" experience that is usually more ephemeral, transitory than the other types. We have already looked at this type of loneliness in its extreme form under "Depression."

In summary then, the causes of loneliness in all its forms seem twofold: the reality of sin, and the frailty of the human condition. In archetypal terms, the story of the tower of Babel (Gen 11) tells of the alienation present in the very fabric of the human condition, a part of the origin of sin, the division, separation among human persons that results from our very frailty. Later the story of Pentecost (Acts 1) tells of the healing of this division by the action of God's spirit, reuniting divided humankind again. Sin divides, separates, creates the varied forms of loneliness. The action of God's spirit re-creates, rebonds, renews.

Hell is only the experience of other people, as it was for Sartre in *No Exit,* when we have not learned to relate to others in a loving, human way. Sin lies at the partial heart of the lonely crowd. If the causes of loneliness are sin and our pilgrim status here in a city that will not endure, then the way out of loneliness or the way to creatively cope with its unavoidability lies in the direction of conversion and an ever-deepening growth into the kingdom of God. Again, every problem at mid-life is a spiritual problem, and loneliness is no exception. We will finally overcome loneliness, or learn to live peacefully with it, by becoming holy people, that is, people in union with God and one another.

Because holiness lies not just in relationship with God, but in ever more loving relationships with one another, this discussion of loneliness leads easily into a consideration of intimacy and sexuality as key dimensions of the task at mid-life.

Note

1. Ronald Rolheiser, *The Loneliness Factor* (Denville, New Jersey: Dimension Books, 1979). This entire book is an excellent treatment of loneliness, but we rely especially on the material in pages 55–90.

4

Intimacy and Sexuality

> It's the heart afraid of breaking, that never learns to
> dance.
> It's the dream afraid of waking that never takes the
> chance,
> It's the one who won't be taken, who cannot seem to
> give,
> And the soul afraid of dying that never learns to live.[1]

Although the issues of intimacy and sexuality obviously endure throughout human life, they assume particular importance, often with incredible power, in mid-life. A
variety of reasons exist for this: the growing sense of mortality that creates the common "last chance" mentality; the
recognition of my destructive capabilities that may drive me
to long for that one perfect, integral relationship; the emptiness of my personal relationships, or my prayer life (or
both), that leave me lonely or empty, and longing for fulfillment. The list could go on, but in one form or another it
would describe the emerging tension between the male and
female *(animus/anima)* parts of ourselves as we struggle to
reconcile this polarity and move into full adulthood.

We are invited to enter into more intense intimacy with
ourselves, first of all, incorporating for the first time the fullness of our human potentiality. As we come to grips with
the shadow side of our own personality, we become less inclined to radically project our needs or desires onto another,
or onto God. This personal integration allows and offers the

opportunity for more honest relationships with others (and with God) than we have ever had before.

As we become more aware of ourselves, we also become aware of our deepest human needs, perhaps disguised or repressed until this time in our lives. We suggest, and deeply believe, that the most fundamental human need is for *intimacy*, not sex. Once we move beyond mere human maintenance—food, sleep, basic material security—we human beings most fundamentally need some sense of union with another (and, again, with God) if we are to be whole, healthy, holy, alive.

It is difficult to describe intimacy because the word has taken on connotations not necessarily inherent in it. We need to say clearly what intimacy is not. Intimacy does not primarily refer either to sexual intercourse or to the vapid facile revelation of my personal self in every inappropriate situation.

We would describe intimacy as the ability to let myself be known by another and to be comfortable in that revelation. Intimacy is the ability, the grace (when appropriate, and in limited relationships) to show myself as I am to another and to trust that that self will be acceptable and accepted.

At the deepest core of my being I need to be known and loved as I am. And the need is a reciprocal one. It is equally important that somewhere in the network of relationships in my life, someone shares with me in trust who he or she is. Intimacy involves the ability to simply be with another, without masks, pretenses, censored conversations, or inhibited reactions. Rarely, if ever, is intimacy a constant state, but it must be experienced with someone, somewhere (and with God) if I am to be whole and at peace.

An excellent description of intimacy as the central human need, distinguished from the necessity of friendship, is provided to us by a mutual friend, a Seattle theologian, George Jeannot. We offer it to you, with his permission.

Friendship and Intimacy

Intimacy is not merely that "at home" feeling with friends, though certainly the experience of friendship is essential for intimacy. We need all the lessons of friendship, whether from elder, or teacher, or peer, to experience intimacy in loving relationships.

A friend is one with whom the other can be comfortable.

An intimate is one with whom the other can be uncomfortable.

A friend is one with whom the other is honest.

An intimate is one with whom the other can be honestly dishonest—who is so closely interbonded into the other's life that the other can play their little games of self-deception while all the time the intimate knows games are being played, and is willing to let them be, so the other can release them. The intimate lets the other work through defensiveness, which devises the game for protection so that defensiveness can be grown through.

A friend is one who draws the other out of crabiness and moodiness, who encourages the recovery of that pleasant aspect which the other truly wants to have.

An intimate is the one who accepts the other in the pleasant aspect, but challenges the other to draw up to the surface the crabiness and moodiness hidden underneath.

A friend is one who remains present with the other in suffering and comforts the other in that suffering.

An intimate is one who suffers with the other in the suffering.

A friend is one who helps the other out of suffering, even if only by helping the other to become reconciled with that suffering.

An intimate is one who gets down into the suffering of the other, who lies on the pavement with the other and feels its hardness and coldness, who experiences the same hurt with which the other cannot at present be reconciled, who hurts in the intensity of the other's hurt, who feels with the other the overwhelming and seemingly insurmountable pain of that hurt.

A friend is one who can appreciate both the other's laughter and tears.

An intimate is one who knows the person who is laughing and crying and can hear the cry in the laughter and the laughter in the cry.

A friend is one who does not leave the other in loneliness, but remains present to encourage moving through the very friendship out of the loneliness.

An intimate is one who knows the other's loneliness and moves through that loneliness and beyond the loneliness to truly becoming alone.[2]

Granted these introductory remarks on intimacy, we must admit that some of the knottiest human problems occur because this desire for intimacy is so easily confused with and feels so much like the drive for genital, sexual union. Certainly intimacy and sexuality are closely allied; our drive for union *is* one drive. Sexuality permeates all of our being, every gesture, every word, every relationship. But sexuality is not the same as the genital expression which ought to be but a part of a larger, much more comprehensive human reality. Our point here is that we often and easily confuse our need for intimacy, certainly a part of our sexual makeup, with the desire for sexual, genital union, which it is not. Everyone knows from human experience that we can have "sex" without intimacy, and intimacy without "sex." What causes the confusion is that so often the drive or longing for honest human intimacy is initially experienced as a genital sexual desire. In fact, Erikson's stages of development, treated earlier in the book, indicate that the capacity for intimacy does not develop in a human being (at least, a male) until the mid-twenties, or several years after puberty, after the possibility for genital expression already exists. We experience the sexual drive before we are capable of the intimacy it masks. And this initial confusion seems to endure well into adulthood, even all our lives.

If Carol Gilligan is correct, and intimacy is a reality for women throughout their development, the confusion that exists between the sexes as they struggle for intimacy is obviously compounded.

This struggle to distinguish the genital drive from the deeper, more humanly significant drive for intimacy seems to endure throughout life. For all the reasons we mentioned before, and many more, the distinction is perhaps only able to be seen for what it is at mid-life. Perhaps only after the frustration of too many meaningless sexual encounters does the reality of one's intimacy need become apparent. Perhaps only after years of repressing one's genital, sexual powers as somehow evil or misguided does one begin to recognize the deeper and irrepressible drive toward intimacy. Perhaps only after years of a "sexually satisfying," but humanly, socially, personally boring marriage does either party begin to realize what he or she truly needed and desired in this relationship.

From whatever part of the spectrum, the individual begins to realize the reality of this intimacy drive; the realization is often a mid-life revelation. The ability to distinguish the sexual drive from our need for intimacy seems a central task of our mid-life transition. We finally come to recognize that intimacy without sexual expression can be nourishing, sustaining, enlivening in our human, spiritual growth, and that genital expression without intimacy dehumanizes and distorts, whether in or out of marriage.

Our book is about spirituality at mid-life, so it is essential that we assert that sexuality and spirituality are very much alike. In his excellent *Will and Spirit*,[3] Gerald May insightfully develops the thesis that the sexual drive and the unitive drive (or the religious impulse) in human beings is the same.

May writes, for example:

Whereas some traditional psychologists maintain that spirituality is nothing but a displacement of human sexuality, it seems to me that even more often human sexuality is a displacement of one's spiritual longings.[4]

And later:

Spiritual passion and erotic passion are so similar that people often find themselves using one as a substitute for the other. The problem is that either way, the substitutions never seem quite right.[5]

And finally:

If the energy that fires both sexual and spiritual feelings is indeed a common "root" force, the distortions of sexuality and spirituality . . . can be seen as resulting not only from confusions about the nature of the longing,

but also from primary misdirections in the processing
of emotional energy.[6]

We desire to be one with another human being and
with God. These two drives interact and overlap. One cannot, May asserts, find union with another person that totally
satisfies our human potential apart from the transcendent
dimension of that unitative desire. Conversely, we cannot
enter into a full union with God that satisfies our human
potential without reference to that incarnate presence of
other human beings that concretize that desire. Intimacy
with God, intimacy with other people, complement, complete, and allow for the possibility of each other.

With the first theologians of our faith, we believe that
the best way to understand the Eucharist, our communion
with Jesus the Lord, is by analogy with the act of sexual love
between committed people in an enduring and endearing
relationship. And sexual love, at its best and most complete,
is most clearly understood in comparison with the union of
Jesus and ourselves in the Eucharist. Both speak of passion,
desire, union, commitment, fidelity. In each we open ourselves to another and accept another into ourselves. In each
there resides a deep nakedness, vulnerability, trust of the
other (yes, Jesus trusts us, as well as we him).

The incorporation of The Song of Songs into the Sacred
Scriptures provides the best sources to assert that God's love
for us is not cerebral, academic, abstract, but, rather, passionate, intense, incarnate. By reason of the strength of our
feelings for one another, our drive for intimacy, we come in
touch with the power of God's love for us and the possible
passion of our love for God. Divorced from an awareness of
our sexual nature, spirituality becomes less than human at
mid-life or any other time.

We do not need to be leading actively genital lives to

come in contact with God's passionate love, but we do need to be in touch with the intensity and power of that force within us, for it is the same drive that leads both to God and toward another human person.

We suggest further that our relationship with God tends to mirror and to be mirrored by our relationship with others. Persons differ on which is prior. For some of us, an intense deep relationship with God, developed through personal or liturgical prayer, leads to more freedom in human relationships and a heightened capacity for human intimacy. For others, the relationships with other human persons will provide an opening, an availability to God's love. Some start with prayer; some are led to prayer. Wherever it begins, a healthy spirituality will complete the circle. Prayer helps us to love; love helps us to pray.

If, through the first half of our lives, we have kept God at a distance, used only formal prayers, were never quite able to be still and let God be God wherever that might lead, we will also have, most probably, kept others at a distance. If we are open, vulnerable, and trusting with God, we will usually be much the same in human relationships.

If we only turn to God in crisis, asking for help, we probably have treated other friends the same way, using them when convenient.

The task of mid-life has been described as one of discovering our androgynous personality. Each of us grows in integrating the feminine and masculine characteristics of our total, balanced personality. A man who lives, works, relates only among other men may well neglect an entire part of his person. So might a woman in an entirely feminine environment. In order to become whole, persons need normal, healthy, regular relationships with both sexes. So every human person needs to develop heterosexual friendships. Celibate priests need women friends to be balanced ministers for all people. Religious women cannot isolate themselves from half the human race and not distort their personalities. Married people need to be enriched by friends of both sexes. Spiritual growth is not divorced from human growth and human growth depends on interaction with both sexes. The balancing of the masculine and feminine in our personalities at mid-life allows for new and creative possibilities as we become more able to diminish the power of projection, expectation, exploitation. Though relationships between the sexes are necessary to reach this integration, the integration itself offers the possibility of deeper, more honestly intimate relationships.

In an article dealing primarily with men and women religious, Peter Cantwell touches on a problem that occurs in marriage and single life as well: the task of contacting and befriending one's repressed sexuality.[7] Anyone who has neglected or repressed the intimacy drive and the sexual drive it contains finds it difficult to pick up the dialogue after twenty years. The ability to enter into honest and deep human relationships, especially with the opposite sex, needs to begin gradually and grow with patience. Sometimes the feeling will be a bit like opening Pandora's box as all the things we had stored deep within come out all at once, far beyond what we had expected. Cantwell offers some guidelines for relationships as one tries a whole new phase of human interaction. First, we need an outside party to talk with in a constant effort to develop one's own sense of personal identity, so necessary for successfully entering into any intimate relationship. He also suggests some reflection questions that seem helpful to anyone exploring a new, and possibly problematic intimate relationship:

> Does this relationship provide a balance of support and challenge? Are both persons able to be honest with each

other as well as genuinely supportive and nurturing? Is there a lot of hidden agenda, of game playing and experimenting going on that neither one is able or willing to bring into the open? If intimacy is the goal, then openness is needed to preserve the integrity of a close . . . friendship.[8]

We end on this note simply to suggest that while intimacy is necessary it is not easy. At mid-life, as all the way along, we learn, grow, and develop gradually as we patiently become more and more at home with ourselves, each other, and our God.

All of the pieces of our brokenness treated in this chapter (Depression, Burn-Out, Loneliness, Intimacy/Sexuality) suggest the growing mid-life need for solitude, personal integration, deep interiority, prayer. Because prayer itself changes, becomes at mid-life itself a problem—or an opportunity—we turn in the next chapter to the subject of prayer.

Notes

1. From "The Rose," Amanda McBroon, © 1977 by Fox Fanfare Music.
2. George Jeannot, "Friendship and Intimacy," an unpublished essay.
3. Gerald May, *Will and Spirit: A Contemplative Psychology* (San Francisco: Harper and Row, 1982). Chapters six and seven on "Love" and "Energy" deal at great length with what is summarized in these pages.
4. *Ibid.,* p. 151.
5. *Ibid.,* p. 154.
6. *Ibid.,* p. 185.
7. Peter Cantwell, "Ongoing Growth Through Intimacy," *Human Development,* Vol. 2, No. 3, Fall 1981, pp. 14–20.
8. *Ibid.,* p. 19.

PART IV

Prayer at Mid-Life

When a woman gives birth to a child, she certainly knows pain when her time comes. Yet as soon as she has given birth to the child she no longer remembers her agony for joy that new life has been born into the world. Now you are going through pain, but I shall see you again and your hearts will thrill with joy—the joy that no one can take away from you (Jn 16:21–22).[1]

The image of childbirth has long been a symbol for the mystery of death/resurrection, not as a single culminating event, but rather as the "stuff" of our daily life and our progressive journey into God. This birth imagery has particular significance, however, for the individual at mid-life. Chronological age is not as important as the psychospiritual experience which heralds the possibility of new life in every aspect of our being.

John's Gospel speaks of the birthing process of each of us, man or woman, when we are called through deeper interiority and receptivity to bring forth our own child (a Jungian symbol of individuation).

When "our time comes" there is indeed wrenching pain as an era of our life ends and a period of disorientation and confusion ensues prior to the bringing forth of the authentic personality, Paul's "hidden self" (Eph 3:17).

The challenge or pain of this stage is sometimes seen as a loss of youth, the awareness of one's mortality. From a Jungian perspective we perceive the central issue as loss of control by the ego in the emergence of the real self. Both of

these are authentic realities. Beneath all symptomatic in-
dications, however, lies the call to a deeper surrender-in-
faith to the living God. Meister Eckhart coined a word for
this birth at the second half of life. He called it "breakthrough."

Eckhart actually speaks of three births within the one
"present now": a birth of our true self in terms of the consciousness of our oneness with God, God's birth of the Son
in us, and our birth as sons and daughters of God.

> Tend only to the birth in you and you will find all good-
> ness and all consolation, all delight, all being and all
> truth. Reject it and you reject all goodness and blessing.
> What comes to you in this birth brings with it pure
> being and blessing. But what you seek or love outside
> of this birth will come to nothing, no matter what you
> will or where you will it.[2]

The dynamics of this surrendering-in-faith which leads
to a new consciousness of our oneness with God initially
seems like a loss of faith for mid-life persons. We can no
longer pray, liturgy seems boring, we feel alienated from
God and others. We are simultaneously disillusioned by
God, the church and ourselves.

> Previously constructed meanings will be cracked by the
> paradox and contradiction of human life. The chal-
> lenge, then, is to undergo this experience, to ride it out,
> to trust ultimately that it is worthwhile and necessary
> for me to walk through the bewildering present into the
> unknown future. This experience teaches me that the
> very essence of faith is to trust that which I cannot
> name.[3]

Because our human experience is its starting point and
content, prayer too is profoundly affected by the upheaval

in our lives. We journey into God as we journey into ourselves. The classics of mystical theology have dealt with this reality but in slightly different terminology. The experience has traditionally been called "the dark night," "the cloud of unknowing," or Merton's "inner experience." Whatever the term, there is the connotation of confusion, vulnerability, paradox and ambiguity. As we learn in faith to face the darkness within, we are able to face the darkness who is God. Our true self can be known only as God is known: apophatically, or in the darkness of the *via negativa*.

This darkness of faith which is of the essence of mid-life is not a capricious God's way of forcing us to let go, much less some means of punishment; rather, it is the gift of a loving God who realizes that faith is the only way in which there can be union. Our human intelligence is simply incapable of comprehending God. Knowledge of God is supra-conceptual, beyond ideas or images. We need the apparent absence of God in order to move beyond our natural ways of knowing and loving. Our attention to God must move beyond the mind to faith expressed in the will. Darkness achieves what years of study cannot. We ultimately know God only by the gift of love which secretly floods our being while conscious life remains in darkness.

It is difficult for us to deal with this darkness and unclarity, one more facet of giving up control. Like Paul we continually kick against the goad (Acts 26:15). The darkness of faith calls for a cessation of our projection onto God of our own image and likeness. In our first chapter we quoted from the letter of a friend: "The pain is that I cannot easily know God . . . when I cannot find God I am desolate and I say that God does not exist. . . . Comfort me! Comfort me!"

Eckhart writes that we are tempted not to let God be God by futilely seeking control in three ways.[4] The first way of seeking control is by trying to name God, to pin God down. The God of Abraham and Sarah, Isaac and Rebekah, Jacob and Rachel and each of us is beyond all categories. God cannot be encompassed by any word in spite of repeated efforts by Moses: "But if they ask me what his name is, what am I to tell them?" (Ex 3:13), by Jacob: "I beg you, tell me your name" (Gen 32:29), and by ourselves. Our attempts to name God are fruitless, largely the result of our own projections. God is beyond masculine or feminine names or images; God is ineffable mystery.

> This God is he who is without name and is the denial of all names and who has never been given a name . . . a truly hidden God. In this way, by reverencing the hiddenness of God, we respect God's transcendence. In this way of the *via negativa* we come to union with the "naked God." And in this kind of union, everything belonging to God belongs to us.[5]

A second way in which we seek to control God is by imagining we can know God intellectually. Just when we feel we have an understanding of who God is, God changes. God is always out "in front" of us. Just when we think we are getting a good look he moves ahead of our vision and perception. Like Moses (Ex 33:23) we see only his "back" or hear God in the "still small voice" (1 Kgs 19:13). Unamuno tells us:

> Those who believe they believe in God, but without passion in the heart, without anguish of mind, without uncertainty, without doubt and even at times without despair, believe only in the idea of God, not in God himself.[6]

It is "knowing" of a different nature that we are invited to. Attention to God is moved from the mind to the will. We move from head to heart. We are called to avoid the ultimate seduction of the mind: understanding.

The whole Hebrew Scriptures stress the mystery and unknowableness of God, God's unlikeness to anything made by human hands or seen by human eyes.

> The Jewish historian Josephus tells the story of how the Roman Pompey, after capturing Jerusalem in 63 B.C., strode into the holy of holies with some of his followers and found there nothing, absolutely nothing. This was the Hebrew way of representing the ineffable nature of Yahweh.[7]

We who are God's holy of holies often feel equally empty at mid-life, feel we have had enough of God. This is a third way of not letting God be God. God pursues us and woos us into infinite mystery. We can never have enough of God precisely because of God's infinite beauty, passion, and energy.

> If you, in fact, could have enough of God, so that there came about a satiety of God in you, then God would not be God.[8]

These attempts at "controlling" God express the desperation and confusion of the mid-life person losing control in all aspects of life. The chaos roughly corresponds to Teresa of Avila's third mansion in the *Interior Castle*. Persons in this stage of the inner journey generally model ordered Christian living with a well-established prayer life, all by way of conscious effort and under ego control. The breakdown of hard-earned discipline and the inflow of the unconscious is a terrifying thing.

In speaking of the dark journey of faith, John of the Cross uses the metaphor of night in its various stages: twilight, mid-night and dawn. Experientially, twilight refers to a period in which we begin to undergo dryness, boredom and a vague dissatisfaction with all forms of prayer and things of the spirit in general. Growth of largely unconscious neurotic anxieties abounds: sexual longings, jealousy, self-pity, insecurity, paranoia, guilt. We are confused, or perhaps further guilt-ridden by the very fact of having these feelings.

Midnight symbolizes the sense of brokenness, failure and even despair that can encompass us. We often experience an overwhelming sense of failure although others perceive us as highly productive, successful and confident. We are weighed down by feelings of helplessness and fragility too painful to articulate to ourselves, let alone another. As one friend put it: "I felt like the village idiot standing on a street corner trying to call out for help, but I couldn't speak and no one paid any attention." God's absence seems total. We feel alienated from ourselves, God and others. There seems to be no light from any source. The essence of this state is that the God-Self has taken over, stripped us of control and subdued the ego. The effect on our conscious life is one of despoliation.

> It [faith] means renouncing myself as my own base, my own centre, my own end. It means so casting myself on another, so making that other my raison d'être that it is, in truth, a death to the ego. The whole of the spiritual journey can be seen in terms of trust, growing in trust until one has lost oneself in God.[9]

Dawn signals some ray of hope and perhaps an intuition that the experience has positive effects, that it is appropriate and all right to be in this desert place. A sense of some unknown interior presence grows great within although we would be hard pressed to articulate this further. Ruth Burrows terms this a "lights off" experience.

> Something unspeakably wonderful is happening in the depth of the self and the self cannot see it. No light shines on it. There are effects flowing from this happening and these are consciously experienced, but not the happening itself.[10]

This phase more or less corresponds to Teresa of Avila's fourth mansion where a new center of peace within the psyche emerges and we move into the prayer of quiet. The stillness and loving openness to God which mark that stage of prayer allow for healing contact with the depths of the self. Her fifth dwelling place moves into the contemplative prayer of union.

In *The Ascent of Mt. Carmel* John of the Cross gives three signs by which to determine if this painfully dry state as experienced in both prayer and life is actually an invitation to a deeper, less conscious form of prayer which he calls "dark contemplation."[11] An authentic invitation calls for an abandonment of meditation which makes active use of mental reflection through images and concepts to mediate an awareness of God. The more passive dark contemplation is thoughtless, even wordless and imageless, trusting totally on God's work in us although we "feel" or perceive nothing of it. There is little for the ego to lay claim to in this form of prayer of faith.

The first criterion given by John is the realization that we simply cannot actively meditate any longer. No satisfaction or success is derived from it no matter how much effort we bring to bear. Prayer is uneventful and arid. Gone are the graced insights and feelings of consolation of an earlier period in life when conscious effort seemed to reap so many blessings.

Second, we feel a kind of repugnance or disinclination to fix our imagination or other sense faculties upon specific objects, interior or exterior. For example, we neither want nor are able to think about or visualize passages of Scripture. This may have been a preferred form of prayer for years and we are confounded or feeling guilty because of our inability. This disinclination to focus carries over in the daily routine. There is a kind of diffuse awareness of our specific reality, a feeling of being "at sea" as a result of being cut loose from a more controlled approach to life and prayer.

The third and surest sign is that we yearn to remain alone in loving awareness of God without dealing with specific topics or agendas. We long for a simple "presence" before God, a being-with rather than thinking about.

Because it could be that the aridity simply follows on negligence or a pattern of sin in our lives, in *The Dark Night* John gives amplifying signs for determining the authenticity of the aridity and inability to "pray" in usual ways as a valid invitation from God to dark contemplation.[12] Not all darkness or dryness of spirit is indicative of progress.

When we undergo this aridity as an authentic call from God, we experience that while the things of God give no consolation, neither does anything else. There is a sense of meaningless—"blahness"—about our life and everything in general. Often we question our life-form (marriage, religious or single life, priesthood). Ministry seems listless and singularly uninspired. In addition, we anguish over displeasing God. Feelings of "wasting time" at prayer cause us to think our attempts fruitless and that God perceives our efforts as we do. Friends or a spiritual director may find it difficult to convince us that our perception of personal prayer is little indication of the authentic value of it.

This transition from a more active, measurable prayer to a dry, uneventful experience is not neat and precise. Pos-

sibly after years of "productive," satisfying prayer we begin
to notice a period of aridity. This aridity increases over time
so that eventually prayer seems to be almost a perpetual
desert state. For some the transition is less gradual.

Initially most of us have a tendency toward constant ex-
amination of conscience to determine what we have done
"wrong." We try even harder. We recognize the same weaknesses of past years when prayer seemed better. In spite of
persistent fragility, God had blessed us enormously, or at
least occasionally. We are confused, puzzled, hurt. Possibly
only then does an insightful book, a perceptive homily, the
intuitive remark of a sensitive friend, or the fruit of silence
bring light to the positive reality of our experience of "non-
prayer."

> In a quiet breathing of love a knowledge is given that is
> to the ego as no knowledge at all. The crucified mind
> knows God without knowing anything. As the ego
> sleeps the inscape of love unfolds within a heart hidden
> in faith. Only by its fruits is it known—an innermost
> thirst for God and a greater capacity to love and be loved
> by others. But in turning to know what one knows, in
> wanting to possess it in a clear idea or feeling, it van-
> ishes in the betrayal of the unity in which it is received.
> This knowledge is not given to a separate self that
> grasps and possesses, but to a surrendered self that
> waits, yields and is transformed.[13]

The critical factor in this faith transition, then, is that
the work of God in the depths of the self hides from the perception of conscious life. Literally, we do not know what is
happening. The ego, center of conscious life, no longer controls the situation. This is a critical time in our relationship
with God, for we feel that an absent God has given up on us.
Many simply forego prayer and a serious journeying in faith

and settle for going through the motions of authenticity, satisfying only conscious myopic expectations which are measurable and safe. The persona remains intact; the ego triumphs once again.

Women and men religious, priests and others involved in church ministry find this a particularly painful time. "Professionals" in the spiritual life are acutely embarrassed and confused by an apparent lack of faith and feel they have failed in ministry because of an inability to pray and to talk easily about God. Honesty about our own struggles and persistence in naked faith is the best ministry we can offer to others.

In this whole crisis, God treasures what seems useless, a waste of time. We are being invited into deeper surrender by the way of non-action called wu-wei in central Asian thinking. A Zen saying sums up rather succinctly what we are called to: "Quit trying, quit trying not to try, quit quitting."

This passively-active stance of the second half of life calls for:

1. Less preoccupation with "doing things" and more ability to let things happen,
2. Less attention to making decisions and more ability to let deepest desires well up to consciousness,
3. Less reasoning and thinking and more intuition and freeing up of deeper regions of the psyche,
4. Less focus on what *I* am unable to do and more attention in faith on the positive thing God is creating in my inner being,
5. Less anxiety about progress in prayer or any other area in my life and more reliance on God's action,
6. Less concern about the quality of any prayer form and a deeper realization that authentic prayer is

found only in the expressed love and concern for others,
7. Less "searching for" God and more awareness of all the places God finds us in our daily life.

In Gerald May's felicitous phrase, we assume a "willing" stance toward life—open, receptive, respectful—rather than a "willful" stance which is grasping, controlling, and manipulative.[14]

The image of floating seems apt. The more relaxed we are, the better. The moment we begin to flail around, the delicate balance between ourselves and the water that surrounds and buoys us up is destroyed. We begin to sink and are left to the devices of our own diminishing energy.[15]

In our success-seeking, production-oriented society with its frantic pace of video games, instant TV replays and prolific computers, it is extremely difficult to passively/receptively wait in the dark. We feel guilty, impotent, as if "spinning our wheels." We almost have to fight down a welling anxiety in order to trust, in faith, that this indeed is what God wants.

> When in empty faith I am doing nothing, a limitless divine love is welling up within me and taking over my life. The emptiness, the void, the darkness—this is infinite love dwelling in the depths of my being. The important thing is that I surrender to this love and allow it to envelop my life.[16]

Eventually, we do begin to perceive the darkness, the desert, as comfortable. We have a sense that although we are doing "nothing" at prayer (at least at the level of sense and intellect) God is working powerfully. Faith intuits that what we do is not nearly as important as what we allow God to do in us.

Not so ironically, at this time when God seems absent in prayer, we need to recognize God's veiled presence more fully outside periods of formal prayer. Personal prayer may be sterile and vapid but situations speak to us of God. People we love and even those unknown speak to us; films, music, drama, art and dance can speak to us. Our unconscious speaks in dreams and fantasy. Every depth experience, whether religious, moral, or artistic, can reveal something of the emerging inner self and the God within who continues to create us.

We have essentially described prayer according to the apophatic tradition, the school of darkness and emptying which holds out imageless contentless prayer as a high point in spiritual growth. We have deliberately chosen this emphasis because this is essentially the vehicle for God's work in us at mid-life.

A second tradition, the cataphatic or school of light, the *via positiva,* emphasizes the use of images and the interior sense of imagination. This hallmark of Ignatian contemplation is also stressed by earlier giants such as Gregory of Nyssa and Augustine. Persons of this orientation profit greatly from guided fantasies and use of active imagination, feelings and sensate or symbolic forms of expression such as art, journaling, weaving, potting, sculpting, dance or musical performance.

As a matter of fact, most people who end up with an apophatic orientation have passed through years of cataphatic experiences on the way. It is not necessarily an either/or situation. The important issue at mid-life is to find our best way to pray, a way that seems compatible with the emerging inner self and God's direction. Neither approach will avoid aridity and periods of the desert, but finding where we seem "at home" (not productive) will avoid unnecessary frustration.

As we have indicated, one of the tasks of mid-life is the reconciling of opposites, the classical "coincidentia oppositorum." This dynamic deals with all aspects of our being: the polarities of masculine/feminine; destruction/creation; attachment/separateness. Prayer is no exception. We begin to see that prayer too is not either/or but both/and. We find that prayer is both active and passive. Within the time of solitude we employ a combination of words or actions as well as silence and stillness, perhaps a simple focusing on our breathing. Prayer is both solitary and personal as well as communal and political. In other words, whether by ourselves or in communal worship, there is a sense not only of relationship with God (at least in faith), but also of our bondedness with all others and concern for their total well-being.

Prayer is also profoundly imminent and profoundly transcendent. At times one is keenly aware of resting in God's presence; at other times, a sense of God's otherness and mysteriousness is almost overwhelming. Contrary to an earlier dichotomizing of prayer and action, we begin to comprehend that there is no time or place where prayer is impossible. All of life becomes prayer. All of human experience can be contemplative, "willing," if we have the eyes of faith.

At some point, we have more awareness of the gift that prayer is, whether it be arid and bleak or consoling and delightful. We realize that while mid-life is often described by words such as emptiness, nakedness, nothingness, or the void, the experience itself is far from negative!

> We must not be afraid of the dark or of the silence or of being without images. Only then are we ready for the secret Word to enter. One reason why silence is so basic to the birth of God (in us) is that the birth takes place from the emptiness of our nothingness. It is such a

pregnancy with nothingness that bears divine fruit. "A man had a dream, a daydream: it seemed to him that he was big with nothingness as a woman is with a child. In this nothingness God was born. He was the fruit of nothingness. God was born in nothingness." Thus the *via negativa* is needed to give birth to God . . . the fruit of letting go is birth.[17]

In our blind groping we realize with increasing certitude that we have already been found.

Finally, we are aware that because prayer and growth are essentially God's work, it must be humbly awaited. We are not in control.

I said to my soul, be still, and wait without hope
For hope would be hope for the wrong thing; wait without
  love
For love would be love of the wrong thing; there is yet faith
But the faith and the love and the hope are all in the
  waiting.
Wait without thought, for you are not ready for thought:
So the darkness shall be the light, and the stillness the
  dancing.
Whisper of running streams and winter lightning.
The wild thyme unseen and the wild strawberry,
The laughter in the garden, echoed ecstasy
Not lost, but requiring, pointing to the agony of death and
  birth.
You say I am repeating
Something I have said before, I shall say it again.
Shall I say it again? In order to arrive there, to arrive where
  you are, to get from where you are not,
You must go by a way wherein there is no ecstasy.
In order to arrive at what you do not know
You must go by a way which is the way of ignorance.
In order to possess what you do not possess

You must go by the way of dispossession.
In order to arrive at what you are not
You must go through the way in which you are not.
And what you do not know is the only thing you know
And what you own is what you do not own
And where you are is where you are not.[18]

Notes

1. *The New Testament*, translated by J.B. Phillips (New York: The Macmillan Co., 1970) p. 240.
2. Meister Eckhart quoted in *Breakthrough* by Matthew Fox (New York: Image Books, 1980) p. 311.
3. James Zullo, "The Crisis of Limits: Midlife Beginnings," *Human Development*, Vol. 3, No. 1, 1982, p. 11.
4. Matthew Fox, *Breakthrough*, pp. 181–85.
5. *Ibid.*, pp. 175–76.
6. This quote is cited without footnote in Kenneth Leech, *True Prayer* (London: Sheldon Press, 1980) p. 136.
7. William Johnston, *The Inner Eye of Love* (New York: Harper & Row, 1978) p. 122.
8. Meister Eckhart quoted in *Breakthrough*, p. 185.
9. Ruth Burrows, *Guidelines for Mystical Prayer* (Denville, N.J.: Dimension Books, 1980) p. 59.
10. *Ibid.*, p. 46.
11. John of the Cross, *The Ascent of Mt. Carmel* in *The Collected Works*, translated by Kieran Kavanaugh and Otilio Rodriguez (Washington, D.C.: ICS Publications, 1973) Book 2, Chap. 13, pp. 140–41.
12. John of the Cross, *The Dark Night, ibid.*, Book 1, Chap. 9, pp. 313–15.
13. James Finley, *The Awakening Call* (Notre Dame: Ave Maria Press, 1984) p. 96.
14. Gerald May, *Will and Spirit* (San Francisco: Harper & Row, 1982) pp. 1–21.
15. Thomas Green, *When the Well Runs Dry* (Notre Dame: Ave Maria Press, 1981) pp. 166–75.

16. William Johnston, *op. cit.*, p. 103.

17. Matthew Fox, *op. cit.*, p. 309, quoting Reiner Schurmann, *Meister Eckhart: Mystic and Philosopher* (Bloomington: University of Indiana Press, 1978) p. 126.

18. T.S. Eliot, "East Coker," *Collected Poems 1909–1962* (New York: Harcourt, Brace and World, Inc., 1963) pp. 186–87.

PART V

Sharing Our Brokenness: Jesus and the Cross

"In your minds you must be the same as Christ Jesus"
(Phil 2:5).

Throughout this book we have offered reflections on spirituality especially during the middle of life. In this final chapter, we will consider more carefully our relationship with Jesus Christ, the central relationship of any Christian spirituality. More specifically, all Christian spirituality is a spirituality of the *cross* and *resurrection* of Jesus. This becomes particularly clear at the time of third-birth, mid-life, dark night, for we are now invited to pass through death to life, to be reborn through a baptism in fire into Christ's death and resurrection.

What Sebastian Moore sees as descriptive of the entire task of life seems, as ought to be evident by this entire book, to be even more cogent at mid-life when what we are tempted to refuse is

> some fullness of life to which God is impelling us and which our whole being dreads. Some unbearable personhood, identity, freedom, whose demands beat on our comfortable anonymity and choice of death. Further, something that at root we *are*, a self that is ours yet persistently ignored in favor of the readily satisfiable needs of the ego. . . . The crucifixion of Jesus then becomes the central drama of man's refusal of his true self.[1]

Before considering this crucifixion of Jesus we offer some *presuppositions* that we hold to be true about all

Christian spirituality. The presuppositions have particular pertinence at mid-life:

1. All life comes out of various kinds of death, "No cross, no crown," "No such thing as a free lunch," or, more profoundly, "Unless the wheat grain falls on the ground and dies, it remains only a single grain; but if it dies, it yields a rich harvest" (Jn 12:24).

2. The experience of mid-life is one of various kinds of death, expressed in various ways, ways we have already spoken of:

Death to youth, and the image of myself as young, eternal, vital, healthy.

Death to youthful idealism and all ideals: I will not be all that I thought I would.

Death to the ego, in the recognition that I am not finally in control of my life, and I need to move from "willfulness," to "willingness," for, finally, I cannot do "it" myself, whatever that "it" may be.

Death to privatism: I am not in this alone, and cannot be the center of my own life.

Death to an excessive sense of community, for paradoxically, I am finally alone before God, responsible for myself.

Death to an image of myself as simply "man" or "woman," for I am (and need to become more) androgynous, incorporating all of myself into myself. The stereotypical macho-man or helpless woman must die.

Death to every image and definition of God, for we discover we can neither contain nor control God by the words we use to describe him.

3. In many human situations the final choice is not whether or not I will suffer, but which suffering can lead to new life, which can lead from chaos to creation.

We cannot always choose the way in which we will be able to avoid suffering, but we can choose how we will suffer, and possibly move through that suffering to new life. The classic choice of an unwed woman facing an unwanted pregnancy offers only difficult choices—abortion, adoption, a much-too-speedy marriage, single-motherhood—each fraught with its own pain. All the options seem bad, all are painful. Often this is the type of choice that characterizes mid-life—to stay in or to leave a marriage of twenty or more years will necessarily be painful; to stay in religious life or the priesthood, or to leave and start life again, will bring pain. Which pain gives the most hope of new life? Out of which death can new life come?

Real death out of which no resurrection, no hope comes usually happens when we naively believe that a choice will not involve suffering (I'll just stay in this marriage and not let it bother me, or I'll get a divorce and then my problems will be over).

On one side we risk the insecurity of starting over with all the accompanying disturbance that can bring. On the other side we risk anger, frustration, or boredom in remaining in and trying to bring the best out of the familiar.

There is, then, pain in staying in the boat and not risking, but that pain may at times be called for. There is pain in getting out and being terrified of the waves, but we may need to do so. In so many human situations we cannot avoid suffering, but we can choose life.

Put another way, when Jesus invites us to take up a cross and follow him (Mt 16:24), it is not always clear which is *my* cross and which is more nearly the cross of Jesus.

4. In all choices in which there is suffering to be undergone on either side, we need to have a strong presumption, a clear bias in favor of what we are already doing, the commitments we have already made. The suf-

fering of living out what I am already committed to (a relationship, a vocation—not necessarily a "job") is more likely to be life-giving.

5. On the other hand, our most basic, initial, and strongest Christian commitment is to baptism, that is, to being a Christian. We need to live out that commitment as best we can. For example, however painful it may be for a man to leave the active ministry of priesthood, he may recognize that it is impossible for him to remain honestly Christian in this life-form. The secondary commitment of priesthood may need to be broken in order to be faithful to that initial call to be a Christian, a loving presence in the world.

6. Out of the experience of mid-life, the words and deeds of Jesus, the ministry and method of Jesus can begin to be understood in new and more vibrant ways by the searching Christian. Before this period of life we really are woefully unequipped to understand what it may mean to lose life in order to save it, to give up one's life for the sake of the Gospel, in order to find that life (Mt 16:24–26). Until we have a "life" to give up, we cannot truly understand the invited surrender. Only in or after mid-life can we begin to understand what it might mean to be "poor in spirit," or "meek," or "peacemaker" (Mt 5:2–10). Only with adequate human experience does the kind of radical suffering involved in the truly Christian life-style begin to ring true.

7. Finally, in these presuppositions about suffering, we repeat what we began with, namely, that it is only in a theology of the cross, a spirituality that involves death and resurrection, that we can adequately frame a spirituality of mid-life.

The above presuppositions form a necessary backdrop to what now becomes the essence of this section, a meditation on Jesus and suffering. We offer this to you as our interpretation of how the reality of Jesus as the Christ for each of us provides the basis of mid-life spirituality. Each reader will nuance these reflections in his or her own way, but finally it is Jesus and his meaning to us as savior that we discover what we have been suggesting in a variety of ways all along, a spirituality for the middle of our lives. This transformation involves on the deepest human level the most dramatic change of our lives. Again, in the words of Sebastian Moore, it is not less than "the transition from [one] 'who crucifies the Lord of Glory' to [one] who is 'nailed to the cross with Christ.' It is the same [person], changing only through self-discovery in Christ."[2]

Ruth Burrows, in her wonderful, small, challenging book, *To Believe in Jesus*, asserts that it is only when we ourselves are stripped and able to look at Jesus without the romanticism that may mark earlier points of our faith journey that we truly encounter Jesus and the possibility of faith:

> There is only one path, the way of the cross. In essence, this means consenting to be taken beyond our limitations, to die that we might live.[3]

And, again:

> The great fundamental question put to us, in which all else is contained, is precisely "do you believe in the Son of Man?" Ultimately it will mean a leap in the dark, for faith always demands that, otherwise it would not be faith but reason working to its conclusions logically.[4]

It is in this spirit that we offer the following meditation.

A MEDITATION ON JESUS AND THE CROSS

In the Philippians hymn with which we began this chapter (Phil 2:5ff) Paul describes the redeeming work of

Jesus as a complete emptying and invites us to have the same "mind" as Jesus. He was equal to God but did not consider that something to be held on to, clutched at; rather he surrendered, emptied himself, took the form of a servant, and became obedient even unto death. He went where he was led, did not hold back, and because of this surrendering, this ultimately "willing" stance toward life, God was able to raise him up and give him a name above every other name. Because of his fully human surrender to God, Jesus becomes the source of our salvation.

The letter to the Hebrews, in its fifth chapter, nuances this theme of obedience in the salvific work of Jesus, for "he learned obedience through the things that he suffered" (Heb 5:8). Jesus became willing through suffering. However distorted this sometimes has become in Christian tradition, it is of great significance that Jesus saves us not because he *died*, but because he was *obedient*. Jesus responded to life as it was, as it presented itself to him, not as he might have wanted it to be. He responded to reality, openly. His stance was not "Why is this happening to me?" but "Since this is happening, how can I most lovingly respond?" We are troubled by the frequent mis-statement of the theology of redemption that implies God's satisfaction, a kind of morbid glee, at Jesus' suffering and death. The reality of "the Father's" joy at Jesus' suffering is not because of the suffering, but because of the integrity, authenticity, "obedience," he showed in entering into and accepting the suffering that came to him.

For example, a mother whose son is an anti-war activist protesting the presence of nuclear submarines in our nation's military arsenal is not pleased that her son goes to jail or even to death for his convictions. She is deeply pleased and proud that he stands up for what he believes and will not back down from his convictions no matter what suffering this may bring.

So it is with the God and Father of our Lord Jesus—not a hand-clapping glee that Jesus suffers so much, but a kind of pride, respect, appreciation for the courage and integrity shown in the way he faces life.

In this understanding, the resurrection becomes the final affirmation by his God that Jesus was right about life, the relative insignificance of death, the totality of the invitation to love. This is what is meant by learning obedience through suffering, coming into the fullness of a human response to suffering "obedientially." Jesus, then, fulfills all that it means to be human, provides the blueprint for full humanness, invites us into the same complete response.

When John begins his Gospel story with a poetic meditation on the "Word made Flesh," he implies by that "flesh" the human person in all its weakness. The eternal Word enters into humanity and specifically into that humanity in all its vulnerability, its capacity to experience suffering, cold, hunger, fear, rejection—all forms of human emptiness. This shared weakness is the beginning and the end of the story of Christian salvation.

Every Scripture reference to the meaning of the life of Jesus implies that this emptying, this vulnerability, this learning of obedience through suffering is finally the point of Jesus' relationship to us. But let us step back from these general theological reflections to look at the concrete specifics of the life of Jesus.

In Luke's Gospel the professed purpose of Jesus' ministry was to relieve suffering. In the fourth chapter of this Gospel, Jesus is led, after baptism and temptation, back to his home town, back to his historic synagogue. Out of the entire Hebrew Scripture, out of the entire Book of Isaiah, he reads a few carefully chosen lines:

The Spirit of the Lord has been given to me,
for he has anointed me.
He has sent me to bring the good news to the poor,
to proclaim liberty to captives,
and to the blind new sight,
to set the downtrodden free,
to proclaim the Lord's year of favor (Lk 4:18; Is. 61:1–2).

Jesus' first public words suggest that this text from the Suffering Servant frames and provides the context for everything he will say or do, for "this text is being fulfilled today even as you listen" (Lk 4:21). The ministry of Jesus was to the suffering dimension of human existence.

In Mark's Gospel Jesus demonstrates a constant care to take away physical pain—"Of course I want to" (Mk 1:42)—even at the expense of himself. He tries to remain anonymous, asks those he cures to refrain from talking about it (e.g., Mk 1:44), in what we refer to as the "messianic secret," knowing full well that they will not, cannot, keep such a silence. In one sense the story of Jesus in Mark is the story of an entire plan failed and his identity revealed too soon, before even his closest followers were able to understand him. The plan fails because Jesus constantly departs from it as he responds to some human person crying out to him in pain.

In each of the Gospels, healing miracles are frequent and diverse. Not every cripple is healed, not every blind person in the world comes to see, but enough occurs to ensure that Jesus takes the body very seriously. The pain, discomfort, limitation that people experienced in their physical being deeply concerned him and he brought the power of love to touch that pain.

He also cared about the moral or psychological pain of people. He touches with a deeper kind of converting love the tax collector who has climbed a tree for a desperate glimpse of him (Lk 19:1–10), the prostitute who trusted him with an entirely different kind of love (Lk 7:36–50), and the woman taken in adultery (Jn 8:1–11). He cared deeply about human suffering in all its forms.

Jesus' constant theme in his preaching was that those who think they have nothing have the kingdom (Mt 5:1–11): the poor, the meek, the peacemakers, the persecuted. Those least likely to believe in and feel worthy of God's love are the ones who have first access to its fullness. Jesus turned the values of his society (and every human society) upside down. This mission of Jesus is the mission of his followers—to invert apparent human values—to afflict the comfortable, and comfort the afflicted. In John's ninth chapter, for example, the blind man comes to see, not just with human eyes, but with the eyes of faith; those who see too well are blind and are convicted because of that blindness.

Jesus' approach to suffering was always paradoxical. He maintained that we do not overcome suffering by running away from it, avoiding it, but by entering into it, embracing it. Thus: "The grain of wheat must die," or "to be worthy of me, take up a cross and follow," or be "poor," "meek," "mourning," "hungering and thirsting for justice," for these are, ironically, the paths to life.

So much of our mid-life passage involves a restructuring of our priorities, our way of seeing things. We have used the language of holding together polarities, or tensions, or the paradoxes of life. Chesterton said somewhere that madness is having everything figured out, but the circle is too small. Sanity and sanctity are cruciform as the truth spreads out in all directions, truths standing in apparent opposition to one another. This mid-life invitation is at the heart of Jesus' understanding of human life.

Another startling paradox invites us both to suffering and to consolation:

Come to me, all you who labor and are overburdened, and I will give you rest. Shoulder my yoke and learn from me, for I am gentle and humble of heart, and you will find rest for your souls. Yes, my yoke is easy and my burden light" (Mt 11:28–30).

Somehow, even in the midst of suffering, our burden is light if it is shared with the Christ who enters into the suffering with us. Thus, so much of our mid-life spirituality consists in inviting others or ourselves into solitude, into prayer, into a patience with the reality we cannot change, into the life of Jesus—not as an answer to our struggles but as a living relationship that frees us to live comfortably with life's questions. It is in kinship, in communion with Jesus, that his followers are empowered to overcome suffering and pain.

This is the heart of John's marvelous image of the vine and the branches (Jn 15:1ff). There will be a pruning for sure, but the branches remaining in him will still bear fruit. After this image, in the second part of the chapter (Jn 15:9–17), John presents Jesus offering us the greatest commandment, the invitation to love, to lay down life for our friends. Again, the invitation is to surrender, to lose control, to lay down life, but "so that my own joy may be in you, and your joy may be complete" (v 11).

Because we have been united with Jesus, because we have known his life, because we are poor and suffering ourselves, we are able to hear the good news. Ironically again, the Gospel of Jesus is preached only to the poor, is only heeded, understood, longed for somehow *in suffering*. Only if we are poor enough to hear this Gospel ourselves are we able to speak anything of the good news to someone else.

Suffering is not just something that Jesus talked about. His life was an incarnation of the Word, and the words he spoke were lived out in his person. An incredible harmony exists between his message and his life.

Throughout the Gospel of Luke, Jesus goes relentlessly where he must go. From the ninth chapter until the passion itself, Jesus moves "toward Jerusalem" despite the death that awaits him there. "There is a baptism I must still receive, and how great is my distress until it is over" (Lk 12:50). All along the way in Luke, as in the other Synoptic Gospels, Jesus predicts the upcoming passion awaiting him. He is able to make this prediction not because he is God, and he wrote the book ahead of time, but because he is human and he is sensitively aware of the forces of evil gathering against him. Somewhat as Martin Luther King, Jr. could foresee his upcoming death in Atlanta if he chose to continue to say what he was saying and do what he was doing in support of striking garbage workers, so Jesus recognizes what must inevitably happen to him. Still he will not turn back, turn away. He chooses to be authentic. He will not deny who he is nor forsake his unique relationship of trust in his God who calls him to act and speak as he does. So Jesus goes on, saying what he believes, doing what he must do, even though it brings more suffering.

Jesus has discovered the secret of suffering, openness to where he is led by life: "Let your will be done, not mine" (Lk 22:43); "Father, into your hands I commit my Spirit" (Lk 23:46)—an absolute trust in God, even in the midst of feeling forsaken.

So throughout his life and until the end, Jesus speaks and lives the central reality at the heart of his own message. Life does come out of death, all the way along and at the end as well. Real *evil* is not pain, not even death, but turning back, giving in to fear, compromising on who I am called to be. Real evil is sin!

Finally, let us look again at the Scripture passage with which we began our reflections on spirituality at mid-life. We recall again the scene of Jesus (who had run the course) with Peter (who had run away). We recall the dialogue: "Do you love me?" "You know I love you." "Feed my lambs."

Writers often imply that these words are addressed by Jesus to Peter only to allow Peter to make up three times for his triple denial. But the profound humanity of Jesus suggests that he wanted, *needed* to know, needed to hear again his friend's profession of love. His sufferings have been borne, and they are bearable, but he wants to know he is loved.

Then Jesus, who needed to know of Peter's love, invites him, and every human being in the middle of life, to live and love and lay down life just as Jesus has.

The final words of Jesus to his friend are the perfect final words of this book, the words of Jesus to us:

> "When you were younger
> you put on your own belt
> and walked where you liked;
> but when you grow old
> you will stretch out your hands,
> and somebody else will put a belt around you
> and take you where you would rather not go. . . ."
> After this he said: "Follow me" (Jn 21:18–19).

This "follow me," constitutes the spirituality of mid-life.

Notes

1. Sebastian Moore, *The Crucified Jesus Is No Stranger* (Minneapolis: The Seabury Press, 1977) p. x.

2. *Ibid.*, p. 7.

3. Ruth Burrows, *To Believe in Jesus* (Denville, New Jersey: Dimension Books, 1978) p. 19.

4. *Ibid.*, p. 6.

Bibliography

Anonymous, *The Cloud of Unknowing*. Baltimore: Penguin Classics, 1973.

Bailey, Raymond. *Thomas Merton on Mysticism*. Garden City: Image Books, 1974.

Beck, Aaron. *The Diagnosis and Management of Depression*. Philadelphia: University of Pennsylvania Press, 1973.

Bergman, Ingmar. *The Marriage Scenarios*. New York: Pantheon Books, 1978.

Bianchi, Eugene C. *Aging as a Spiritual Journey*. New York: Crossroad, 1982.

Bloom, Anthony. *Beginning To Pray*. New York: Paulist Press, 1970.

———. *Courage To Pray*. New York: Paulist Press, 1973.

Block, Marilyn, *et al*. *Women Over Forty: Visions and Realities*. New York: Springer, 1980.

Brewi, Janice and Brennan, Anne. *Mid-Life: Psychological and Spiritual Perspectives*. New York: Crossroad, 1982.

———. *Mid-Life Directions*. New York: Paulist Press, 1985.

Bridges, William. *Transitions*. Menlo Park: Addison Wesley, 1980.

Burns, David. *Feeling Good*. New York: Signet, 1981.

Burrows, Ruth. *Guidelines for Mystical Prayer*. Denville: Dimension Books, 1980.

———. *To Believe in Jesus*. Denville: Dimension Books, 1978.

Cantwell, Peter. "Ongoing Growth Through Intimacy," *Human Development*, Vol. 2, No. 3, Fall 1981. pp. 14–20.

Carroll, L. Patrick, and Dyckman, Katherine. *Inviting the Mystic: Supporting the Prophet.* New York: Paulist Press, 1981.

———. *Solitude to Sacrament.* Collegeville: Liturgical Press, 1982.

Caulfield, Sean. *The Experience of Praying.* New York: Paulist Press, 1980.

———. *In Praise of Chaos.* New York: Paulist Press, 1981.

Conway, James. *Men in Midlife Crisis.* Elgin: Cook Pub., 1978.

———. *You and Your Husband's Midlife Crisis.* Elgin: Cook Pub., 1980.

de Castillejo, Irene. *Knowing Woman.* New York: Harper and Row, 1973.

De Rosis, Helen and Pellegrino, V. *The Book of Hope: How Women Can Overcome Depression.* New York: Bantam, 1978.

Eliot, T.S. *The Complete Poems & Plays 1909–1950.* New York: Harcourt, Brace & World, 1962.

Erikson, Erik. *Childhood and Society.* New York: Norton & Norton, 1950 (1963).

———. "Identity and The Life Cycle," *Psychological Issues,* Vol. 1, No. 1 (Monograph), 1959.

Evans, Donald. *Struggle and Fulfillment.* New York: William Collins Pub., 1979.

Finley, James. *Merton's Palace of Nowhere.* Notre Dame: Ave Maria Press, 1978.

———. *The Awakening Call.* Notre Dame: Ave Maria Press, 1984.

Fowler, James. *Becoming Adult, Becoming Christian.* San Francisco: Harper and Row, 1984.

———. *Stages of Faith.* New York: Harper and Row, 1981.

——— and Keen, Sam. *Life Maps.* Waco: Word Books, 1978.

Fox, Matthew. *Breakthrough: Meister Eckhart's Creation Spirituality in New Translation*. New York: Doubleday and Co., 1980.

———. *On Becoming a Musical Mystical Bear*. New York: Paulist Press, 1978.

———. *A Spirituality Named Compassion*. Minneapolis: Winston Press, 1979.

Freudenberger, Herbert J. *Burn-Out*. New York: Bantam, 1980.

Fuchs, E. *The Second Season—Life, Love and Sex: Women in the Middle Years*. Garden City: Anchor Press, 1977.

Gelpi, Donald. *Experiencing God—A Theology of Human Emergence*. New York: Paulist Press, 1978.

Gill, James. "A 1980 Look at Depression," *Human Development*, Vol. 1, No. 1, Spring 1980, pp. 21–27.

Gilligan, Carol. *In a Different Voice*. Cambridge: Harvard University Press, 1983.

Goldbrunner, Josef. *Individuation: A Study of the Depth Psychology of Carl Gustav Jung*. Stanley Godman, trans., New York: Pantheon, 1956.

Gould, R.L. "The Phases of Adult Life: A Study in Developmental Psychology," *American Journal of Psychiatry*, Vol. 129, November 1972, pp. 33–43.

Grant, Harold, *et al. From Image to Likeness: A Jungian Path In the Gospel Journey*. New York: Paulist Press, 1983.

Green, Thomas. *When the Well Runs Dry*. Notre Dame: Ave Maria Press, 1979.

———. *Darkness in the Marketplace*. Notre Dame: Ave Maria Press, 1980.

Griffin, Emile. *Turning: Reflections on the Experience of Conversion*. New York: Image Books, 1982.

Harding, Esther. *The Way of All Women*. New York: Harper and Row, 1970.

Hays, Edward. *Pray All Ways*. Easton: Forest of Peace Books, 1981.

Hillman, James. *Insearch*. Dallas: Spring Pub., 1967.

Hopkins, Gerard Manley. *A Hopkins Reader*. Garden City: Image Books, 1966.

John of the Cross. *The Collected Works*. Translated by K. Kavanaugh and O. Rodriguez. Washington: ICS Pub., 1973.

Johnston, Robert. *He*. New York: Harper and Row, 1977.

———. *She*. New York: Harper and Row, 1976.

———. *We*. New York: Harper and Row, 1983.

Johnston, William. *The Inner Eye of Love*. New York: Harper and Row, 1978.

———. *Silent Music*. New York: Harper and Row, 1974.

Jung, Carl Gustav. *Collected Works*. Translated by R.F.C. Hull. Bollingen Series XX. Vol. 8: *The Structure and Dynamics of the Psyche*. Princeton: Princeton University Press, 1969.

———. *Collected Works*. Translated by R.F.C. Hull, Bollingen Series XX. Vol. 9i: *The Archetypes and The Collective Unconscious*. Princeton: Princeton University Press, 1959.

Keen, Sam. *To a Dancing God*. New York: Harper and Row, 1970.

Kelsey, Morton. *The Other Side of Silence*. New York: Paulist Press, 1976.

———. *Transcend: A Guide to the Spiritual Quest*. New York: Crossroad, 1981.

Kraft, William. *Achieving Promises: A Spiritual Guide for the Transitions of Life*. Philadelphia: Westminster Press, 1981.

———. "Nothingness and Psycho-Spiritual Growth," *Review For Religious*, Vol. 37, November 1978, pp. 866–81.

Leech, Kenneth. *True Prayer*. San Francisco: Harper and Row, 1980.

Le Guin, Ursula. *A Wizard of Earthsea*. New York: Bantam, 1977.

Leonard, Linda. *The Wounded Woman: Healing the Father-Daughter Relationship*. Boulder: Shambhala Pub., 1982.

Levinson, Daniel, *et al*. *The Seasons of a Man's Life*. New York: Alfred A. Knopf, 1978.

Lindberg, Anne Morrow. *Gift from the Sea*. New York: Vintage Books, 1965.

Linn, Dennis and Matt. *Healing Life's Hurts*. New York: Paulist Press, 1978.

Loder, James. *The Transforming Moment: Understanding Convictional Experiences*. San Francisco: Harper and Row, 1981.

Lowen, Alexander. *Depression and the Body*. New York: Penguin Books, 1980.

May, Gerald. *Care of Mind, Care of Spirit*. San Francisco: Harper and Row, 1982.

―――. *Will and Spirit: A Contemplative Psychology*. San Francisco: Harper and Row, 1982.

Mayer, Nancy. *The Male Mid-Life Crisis*. New York: Viking Press, 1978.

Main, John. *Word into Silence*. New York: Paulist Press, 1981.

Maloney, George, *Inward Stillness*. Denville: Dimension Books, 1974.

McConnell, A. *Single After Fifty*. New York: McGraw-Hill, 1978.

Merton, Thomas. *The Strange Islands*. New York: New Directions Books, 1957.

―――. *Contemplation in a World of Action*. New York: Doubleday, 1973.

Miller, Jean Baker. *Toward a New Psychology of Women.* Boston: Beacon Press, 1976.

Moore, Sebastian, *The Crucified Jesus Is No Stranger.* Minneapolis: Seabury Press, 1977.

Moustakas, Clark. *Loneliness and Love.* New York: Prentice-Hall, 1972.

Murphy, Sheila, *Midlife Wanderer: The Woman Religious in Mid-life Transition.* Whitinsville: Affirmation Books, 1983.

Nelson, James. *Embodiment.* Minneapolis: Augsburg Pub., 1978.

Nouwen, Henri. *Reaching Out.* New York: Doubleday, 1975.

————. *With Open Hands.* Notre Dame: Ave Maria Press, 1972.

O'Collins, Gerald. *The Second Journey.* New York: Paulist Press, 1978.

O'Connor, Elizabeth. *Search for Silence.* Waco: Word Books, 1972.

Pennington, Basil. *Daily We Touch Him.* New York: Doubleday, 1979.

Raine, Kathleeen. *The Collected Poems of Kathleen Raine.* New York: Random House, 1956.

Rizzuto, Ana-Maria. *The Birth of the Living God.* Chicago: University of Chicago Press, 1979.

Roberts, Bernadette. *The Experience of No-Self.* Sunspot: Iroquois House Pub., 1982.

Rolheiser, Ronald. *The Loneliness Factor.* Denville: Dimension Books, 1979.

Rossner, Judith. *August.* New York: Warner Books, 1981.

Rubin, L.B. *Intimate Strangers.* New York: Harper and Row, 1983.

————. *Women of a Certain Age: The Midlife Search for Self.* New York: Harper and Row, 1979.

Sammon, Sean. "Life After Youth: The Mid-Life Transition, and Its Aftermath," *Human Development,* Vol. 3, No. 1, Spring 1982, pp. 15–25.

Sanford, John. *Evil: The Shadow Side of Reality.* New York: Crossroad, 1982.

———. *Invisible Partners.* New York: Paulist Press, 1980.

———. *The Kingdom Within.* New York: Lippincott Co., 1970.

———. *Ministry Burnout.* New York: Paulist Press, 1982.

Sarton, May. *Selected Poems.* New York: Norton, 1978.

Scarf, Maggie. *Unfinished Business.* New York: Doubleday, 1980.

Schmidt, J. *Praying Our Experiences.* Winona: St. Mary's College Press, 1980.

Shannon, William H. *Thomas Merton's Dark Path.* New York: Farrar Straus Giroux, 1981.

Shea, John. *The Hour of the Unexpected.* Niles, Ill.: Argus, 1977.

Sheehy, Gail. *Passages.* New York: Bantam Books, 1977.

———. *Pathfinders.* New York: Bantam Books, 1982.

Spencer, Anita. *Seasons: Women's Search for Self Through Life Stages.* New York: Paulist Press, 1982.

Stein, Murray. *In Midlife: A Jungian Perspective.* Dallas: Spring Pub., 1983.

Studzinski, Raymond. *Spiritual Direction and Midlife Development.* Chicago: Loyola University Press, 1985.

Teresa of Avila, *The Collected Works,* Vol. 1. Washington: ICS Pub., 1976.

———. *The Collected Works,* Vol. 2. Washington: ICS Pub., 1980.

Tournier, Paul. *The Seasons of Life.* Richmond: John Knox Press, 1965.

———. *Learn To Grow Old.* New York: Harper and Row, 1972.

Ulanov, Ann Belford. *Receiving Woman: Studies in the Psychology and Theology of the Feminine.* Philadelphia: Westminster Press, 1981.

———. "The Self as Other," *Journal of Religion and Health,* Vol. 12, April 1973, pp. 140–68.

Vaillant, George. *Adaptation to Life.* Boston: Little, Brown, 1977.

Van Kaam, Adrian. *The Transcendent Self.* Denville, New Jersey: Dimension Books, 1979.

Welch, John. *Spiritual Pilgrims: Carl Jung and Teresa of Avila.* New York: Paulist Press, 1982.

Whitehead, Evelyn and James. *Christian Life Patterns: The Psychological Challenges and Religious Invitation of Adult Life.* New York: Doubleday, 1979.

———. *Seasons of Strength: New Visions of Adult Christian Maturing.* New York: Doubleday, 1984.

Zullo, James. "The Crisis of Limits and Midlife Beginnings." *Human Development.* Vol. 3, No. 1, Spring 1982, pp. 6–14.